Wordsworth's Imagery

A STUDY IN POETIC VISION

by Florence Marsh

ARCHON BOOKS
HAMDEN   LONDON
1963

[*Yale Studies in English, Vol. 121*]

Library of Congress Catalog Number: 63-16551

To Professor Frederick A. Pottle

Prefatory Note

THIS BOOK consists of a series of related essays centering about Wordsworth's imagery. I have not hoped in them to contribute to biographical data nor to develop minute analyses of separate poems; I have hoped to contribute to knowledge of Wordsworth's imaginative world. The first of these essays, a general theoretical discussion of the interrelationships of language, poetry, and imagery, provides the basis for the study as a whole and enables us to consider Wordsworth in a wider perspective. The theory of symbolism developed in the first chapter provides the basis for Chapters III, IV, and V, which develop in some detail the significance in Wordsworth's poetry of the seemingly literal that is really a vehicle. Chapter II deals briefly with metaphor and simile in Wordsworth's poetry; Chapter VI deals briefly with the imaginative failure evident in the late poetry. The final chapter attempts an exposition of Wordsworth's own theory of imagery. These essays enable us to approach an important poet from a new direction and simultaneously to gain additional insight into the nature and function of imagery.

This book in its original form was presented to the faculty of the Graduate School of Yale University in candidacy for the degree of Doctor of Philosophy. The study was done under the direction of Frederick A. Pottle; his patience, kindness, and encouragement have been a help in time of trouble. I am also indebted to William K. Wimsatt, Douglas Knight, Cleanth Brooks, and Laurence Michel, all of whom made suggestions concerning revision of the original manuscript, and to Benjamin Nangle for guidance in its final preparation.

May, 1952
Western Reserve University

Contents

Bibliographical Note

The Poetical Works of Wordsworth, edited by Thomas Hutchinson (London, Oxford University Press, 1942), has been used as the standard text for all references to Wordsworth's poetry with the exception of the *juvenilia, The Recluse,* and *The Prelude.* The *juvenilia* are to be found only in the first volume of *The Poetical Works of William Wordsworth,* edited by Ernest de Selincourt (Oxford, Clarendon Press, 1940). References to *The Recluse* are to the fifth volume of this same edition, edited by Ernest de Selincourt and Helen Darbishire (Oxford, Clarendon Press, 1949). References to *The Prelude* are to the comparative edition edited by Ernest de Selincourt (Oxford, Clarendon Press, 1926). Since the 1850 version of *The Prelude* is the version readily available to most readers, quotations are from that text except when Wordsworth's revisions necessitate the use of the earlier version. My practice may seem inconsistent, but I have used the 1805 text only when the point being discussed could be shown only in that version. In footnote references to *The Prelude,* "A" indicates the 1805 text; "MS" references are those available only in De Selincourt's notes and not separately published. I have italicized the titles of all poems and have put in quotation marks first lines of poems that have no titles.

The following cue titles are used:
Diary: Diary, Reminiscences, and Correspondence of Henry Crabb Robinson. Thomas Sadler, ed. London, 1869. 3 vols.
EL: The Early Letters of William and Dorothy Wordsworth. Ernest de Selincourt, ed. Oxford, Clarendon Press, 1935.
IF: Notes dictated by Wordsworth to Isabella Fenwick. These can be found either in *Prose Works, 3,* or throughout the notes in *PW.*
LY: The Letters of William and Dorothy Wordsworth, the Later Years. Ernest de Selincourt, ed. Oxford, Clarendon Press, 1939. 3 vols.
MY: The Letters of William and Dorothy Wordsworth, the Middle Years. Ernest de Selincourt, ed. Oxford, Clarendon Press, 1937. 2 vols.
PW: The Poetical Works of William Wordsworth. Ernest de Selincourt and Helen Darbishire, ed. Oxford, Clarendon Press, 1940–49. 5 vols.
Prose Works: The Prose Works of William Wordsworth. Alexander B. Grosart, ed. London, 1876. 3 vols.

I

Image and Idea: A Theory of Symbolism

STUDY OF WORDSWORTH'S IMAGERY presents at the outset certain difficulties. Current critical theory which defines imagery in terms of metaphor does not seem to apply. Confronted with the paradox of a major poet whose imagery yields almost nothing for discussion, the student is faced with the choice of one of two alternatives: either the poet has been overestimated or the terms of the student's own definitions are wrong. The New Critics, approaching the Romantic poets with terms drawn from metaphysical imagery, have by and large taken the first choice—the poets are at fault.[1] The second alternative has seemed to me worth exploring.

While discussions of imagery in terms of metaphor are not useful in study of Wordsworth's imagery, other theories, postulating the undifferentiated nature of poetic language and the intuitive quality of poetic thought and leading into a theory of symbolism, do prove useful. Therefore in this chapter I wish to consider the fundamental interrelationships of language, poetry, and imagery in order to arrive at a theory of symbolism which will provide the basis for this study as a whole.[2] Since language, poetry, and imagery seem like circles within circles—language the outermost, all-encompassing circle and imagery the innermost core —a brief consideration of language and poetry should not lead us hopelessly astray but should make clearer both the nature of imagery itself and the connection between imagery and ideas in poetry.

Language, it is now generally recognized, has in its evolution become less poetic; as Jespersen put it, "The evolution of language shows a progressive tendency from inseparable irregular conglomerations to freely and regularly combinable short elements."[3] These "inseparable irregular conglomerations" were by their very nature poetic: they were

1. John Crowe Ransom, "William Wordsworth: Notes toward an Understanding of Poetry," in *Wordsworth: Centenary Studies Presented at Cornell and Princeton Universities*, ed. Gilbert Dunklin (Princeton, Princeton University Press, 1951), pp. 91–113, is a most notable exception.

2. Richard H. Fogle in his chapter "Romantic Bards and Metaphysical Reviewers," in his *The Imagery of Keats and Shelley* (Chapel Hill, University of North Carolina Press, 1949), pp. 241–78, while summarizing the generally negative attitude of contemporary criticism to Romantic poetry, fails to arrive at a synthesis which in any way relates the nature of Romantic poetry to the nature of the poetry which recent critics favor. The present chapter may perhaps provide such a synthesis.

3. Otto Jespersen, *Language, Its Nature, Development, and Origin* (London, Allen & Unwin, 1933), p. 429.

creations of the mind and they were living wholes. According to Cassirer's *Language and Myth,* language, art, religion, and all symbolic forms have developed as precipitations in moments of intense consciousness from a previously undifferentiated whole. None of the symbolic forms, in Cassirer's opinion, "arise initially as separate, independently recognizable forms, but every one of them must first be emancipated from the common matrix of myth." [4] The original function of language is believed to have been not communication but simply a naming or way of *"holding on to the object"* by means of a symbol.[5] Since the first symbols were undifferentiated, they contained in themselves an imaginative unity. They were not metaphoric to their makers, since primitive consciousness naturally experienced reality in perceptual wholes; later, more rational consciousness finds these first primitive creations metaphoric since they fuse elements of experience now regarded as disparate. Metaphor is thus, as Gertrude Buck says, "the necessary stage through which speech must pass on its way to literalism." [6]

I. A. Richards has termed metaphor "the omnipresent principle of language." [7] It would seem more accurate to say that metaphor is the creative principle in language, allied to the original creative force which in primitive times first precipitates the spoken symbol. Cassirer differentiates sharply between metaphor as a *"conscious* denotation of one thought content by the name of another which resembles the former in some respect, or is somehow analogous to it," and genuine "radical" metaphor which is a new creation occurring as a resolution of inner excitement and involving much more than a "bare substitution." Cassirer implies that true metaphor as opposed to mere rhetoric always involves this process of "concentration, the compression of given sense experiences, which originally initiates every single verbal concept." [8] Buck in her study of metaphor shows how the poet, like the savage and the child, often has not two things in his thought but only one. Often in poets, she says, "utterance takes place when the two elements in the perception are just emerging from the primitive mass." [9] In other words, the creation of a poetic metaphor is very like the creation of language itself.

In addition to this creative, unifying force, a second force functions in language—the rational or analytic which splits up the original un-

4. Ernst Cassirer, *Language and Myth,* tr. Susanne K. Langer (New York, Harper, 1946), p. 44.

5. Susanne K. Langer, *Philosophy in a New Key* (Cambridge, Harvard University Press, 1942), pp. 132–5. See also Cassirer, pp. 23–43.

6. Gertrude Buck, *The Metaphor, a Study in the Psychology of Rhetoric,* Contributions to Rhetorical Theory, 5 (Ann Arbor, Inland Press, 1899), p. 69. See also Jespersen, pp. 431–2.

7. Ivor A. Richards, *The Philosophy of Rhetoric* (New York, Oxford University Press, 1936), p. 92.

8. Cassirer, pp. 94–5.

9. Buck, p. 33.

differentiated meanings into increasingly differentiated meanings and leads to the development of exact meaning. As D. G. James says in his summary of Kant, "all our knowledge shows these two sides, the direct and imaginative, prehending individual wholes; the reflective or discursive, analyzing and classifying." [1] Owen Barfield compares the "ascending rational principle and the descending poetic principle" to two buckets in a well, each creating its own kind of universal. Poetic universals were the "old, concrete, unitary meanings" which seemed real and alive; abstract universals are general ideas arrived at by abstraction which seem lifeless and mere intellectual conveniences.[2] Exact scientific discourse in which the meaning of words comes closest to being absolutely determined comes as a very late development in language as the product of a long period of increasing abstraction of general meanings out of the early undifferentiated meanings. Thus, while poetry attempts to restore the freshness of consciousness and the awareness of the world as a living unity, science abstracts and isolates, and its syntheses are classifications of abstractions. Theoretical, discursive thought, as Cassirer says, "tends towards expansion, implication and systematic connection"; it extends clarity to wider and wider areas, relating specimen to species to genus.[3] Poetic thought, like mythic thought, concentrates and heightens experience, aiming at intensity rather than clarity.

Words themselves function differently in the two kinds of thought. Scientific discourse aims at giving words fixed meanings independent of their context; poetry continually redefines the meanings of words by the context in which they are used and at its best creates new meaning. For normal language the scientific ideal is something of an impossibility: the meaning of any word is less an absolute fixed content than a function of the word determined by the other terms with which it appears.[4] Richards defines a word as "a permanent set of possibilities of understanding"; [5] one questions the "permanent" since some of the possibilities seem to disappear as new ones develop. Metaphor is to a

1. *Scepticism and Poetry: An Essay on the Poetic Imagination* (London, Allen & Unwin, 1937), p. 23.

2. *Poetic Diction, a Study in Meaning* (London, Faber & Gwyer, 1928), pp. 84–5. See also pp. 73–4 where Barfield calls the poetic force "the principle of living unity" and the analytic force simply the "non-poetic." See also Thomas Clark Pollock, *The Nature of Literature: Its Relation to Science, Language, and Human Experience* (Princeton, Princeton University Press, 1942), pp. 94–103, 141. Pollock differentiates between the language of science which "communicates not the actual reality of human experience (E) itself, but only refers to generalizations abstracted from human experience (E)" and the language of literature which he terms "evocative" rather than "referential."

3. Cassirer, *Language and Myth*, pp. 56 ff., 88 ff., 90–1.

4. See Langer, *Philosophy in a New Key*, chaps. iii–v; Richards, *The Philosophy of Rhetoric*, pp. 47–65; Alan H. Gardiner, *The Theory of Speech and Language* (Oxford, Clarendon Press, 1932), pp. 50 ff.

5. Ivor A. Richards, "The Interactions of Words," in *The Language of Poetry*, ed. Allen Tate (Princeton, Princeton University Press, 1942), p. 73.

large extent responsible for this life in language, this constant growth of meaning which makes words resist an absolute fixed content.

Language, then, in its historical development has been a radiation out from a central core of undifferentiated meaning. In its origin language was identical with the innermost circle that is at once literal and figurative meaning, but in its growth and development words have tended to lose their original concentrations of meaning and to divide into separate and discrete meanings. As long as the meanings of individual words remained concrete wholes, language was naturally poetic. As the development of language split individual meanings, language led away from the poetic toward the scientific.[6] The growth of language seems to reveal some kinship between the undifferentiated and the poetic: as the concrete totalities symbolized in early words were lost to view, poetry, having less in the nature of words themselves to facilitate it, became more and more a conscious creation rather than a spontaneous expression.

It does not follow, however, as Peacock thought, that poetry inevitably had its fullest expression in primitive times and must disappear as a consequence of the growth of science. True, the poetic view of life has become more difficult but therefore more valuable. The poet restores language to its original function, making of it a symbol to name or objectify experience. To say that the use is primitive makes it more rather than less important: poetry, like earliest language, satisfies a basic, elemental need of the mind.[7] The kinship between religion and poetry that has been often recognized and often decried seems to me to lie in the fact that both give insights into relationships, a vision of the nature of things.

Nor does it follow that rational, analytic thought has no part in poetry. Scientists subordinate the imagination to the checks and tests of the critical intelligence; poets keep the critical intelligence working in

6. See Jespersen, *Language*, p. 437: "In primitive picture-writing, each sign meant a whole sentence or even more—the image of a situation or of an incident being given as a whole; this developed into an ideographic writing of each word by itself; this system was succeeded by syllabic methods, which had in their turn to give place to alphabetic writing. . . . Just as here the advance is due to a further analysis of language, smaller and smaller units of speech being progressively represented by single signs, in an exactly similar way, though not quite so unmistakably, the history of language shows us a progressive tendency towards analyzing into smaller and smaller units that which in the earlier stages was taken as an inseparable whole." See also p. 431, where Jespersen comments on the relationship of language development to poetry and prose. Recent language is better adapted to express abstract things and has greater clarity and pliancy; the old concrete words, however, were better adapted to poetic purposes because they would at once present the image "as an indissoluble whole."

See also Wilbur Marshall Urban, *Language and Reality: The Philosophy of Language and the Principles of Symbolism* (London, Allen & Unwin, 1939), p. 459: "the first apprehension of things—and the forms in which it was communicated—have the essentially poetic character."

7. See the discussion in James, *Scepticism and Poetry*, chap. i, of the imagination as operative in all knowledge of the world. The fact that we see an object as object, not as unrelated color, shape, etc., is evidence of the imagination as basic activity of the mind.

combination with, but subordinate to, the imaginative vision. Wallace Stevens observes that the imagination changes as the mind changes. Given a simple person, the imagination is simple. "But given another mind, given the mind of a man of strong powers, accustomed to thought, accustomed to the essays of the imagination, and the whole imaginative substance changes. . . . The primitivism disappears. The Platonic resolution of diversity appears. The world is no longer an extraneous object, full of other extraneous objects, but an image." [8]

What does follow is that poetry like primitive language creates a concrete totality. Science, as Whitehead has pointed out, destroys the unity of the world.[9] The function of poetry is to *"restore* this unity conceptually, after it has been lost from perception." [1] Primitive language *seems* poetic because its units of meaning are undifferentiated; a child's language *seems* poetic because the child too holds together elements that adult minds separate.[2] Both seem poetic to adult analytic consciousness, which perceives not only concrete particularity but, fused with it, a more general significance. The distinctive quality of the poetic intuition is that in its concrete particularity it is still a totality—more than concrete and more than particular. If the concrete totality symbolizes a child's vision, the result will be poetry but obviously poetry of a limited value—the vision will not include enough. Only as the concrete totality is the vision of a mature mind, including the heights and depths of being, is satisfying poetry created. Great poets more than other persons do somehow see a oneness in things that to analytic consciousness are disparate. C. D. Lewis does well in calling attention to the remarkable agreement among English poets "that poetry's truth comes from the perception of a unity underlying and relating all phenomena, and that poetry's task is the perpetual discovery, through its imaging, metaphor-making faculty, of new relationships within this pattern, and the rediscovery and renovation of old ones." [3]

Whereas the symbols of primitive language were single clusters of meaning, the poetic symbol proper—the poem—is not one word but a complex of words which taken together name or define the experience of the poet. His poem like the primitive's word is essentially a creation and a naming—a symbol that enables the poet to hold on to his experience and to communicate it to others. It is admittedly impractical;[4] its

8. "Imagination as Value," in *English Institute Essays, 1948,* ed. D. A. Robertson, Jr. (New York, Columbia University Press, 1949), pp. 20–1.
9. Alfred North Whitehead, *Science and the Modern World* (Cambridge, The University Press, 1926), pp. 78, 104.
1. Barfield, *Poetic Diction,* p. 73.
2. A child speaks of a horse *rocking* its tail.
3. Cecil Day Lewis, *The Poetic Image* (London, Jonathan Cape, 1947), p. 34.
4. See Max Eastman, *Enjoyment of Poetry, with Other Essays in Aesthetics* (New York, Scribners, 1939), pp. 3–24; Frederick A. Pottle, *The Idiom of Poetry* (Ithaca, Cornell University Press, 1946), pp. 67–9; John Crowe Ransom, *The New Criticism* (Norfolk, Conn., New Directions, 1941), p. 226.

function is neither to indoctrinate nor to realize emotion but to capture and hold experience. Like the spoken word the poem is a creative symbol, precipitated in moments of intense consciousness from previously unnamed experience. Early language sprang from an undifferentiated consciousness that saw things whole and therefore seems poetic; poetry strives to return us to the vision of things whole at a higher, conscious level.

The clue to the relationship between imagery and ideas seems to lie in the relationship of language and imagery. If language in its poetic stage is undifferentiated, the corollary seems to be that thought in its poetic stage is likewise undifferentiated and whole. One expects to find ideas in poetry expressed not in the exact literal statement that results from analysis but in language that will leave the idea latent in the image. Once ideas have broken up so that they can be expressed literally, the imaginative life and the unity that seem to be natural poetry have died out and the ideas belong to—or are moving toward—science. Examination in turn of the poetry of things and the poetry of ideas may make the nature of poetic thought even clearer. Since Wordsworth is regarded by an important contemporary critic as hostile to thought in poetry, it is necessary to have the nature of poetic thought clearly before us.[5]

The poetry of things is, I think, closely connected with recent discussions of "pure poetry" which have attempted to distinguish between the purely aesthetic and the aesthetic given added theoretic value. The connection is suggested by George Moore, whose *An Anthology of Pure Poetry* takes as its criterion "something that the poet creates outside of his own personality" containing "no hint of subjectivity."[6] The amazingly concrete and literal quality of his selections,[7] taken in combination with his distaste for poetry "sicklied oe'r with the pale cast of thought" and with his feeling that "at the heart of poetry" the poet deals not with ideas but with "the only permanent world, the world of things," seems to indicate that his "pure poetry" involves the identification of poetry with the concrete or "purely" aesthetic. In Moore's opinion most of Shakespeare's songs are "never soiled . . . with thought."[8]

This distinction between poetry which deals simply with what Whitehead calls "concrete particular realities"[9] and poetry which adds criticism of life appears most clearly in the chapter entitled "Pure Poetry in Theory and Practice" in Frederick Pottle's *The Idiom of Poetry*. Pot-

5. Cleanth Brooks, *Modern Poetry and the Tradition* (Chapel Hill, University of North Carolina Press, 1939), pp. 6–10.

6. (New York, Horace Liveright, 1925), pp. 34–5.

7. See for example Marlowe's *The Passionate Shepherd to His Love,* Shakespeare's *When Daisies Pied,* Ben Jonson's *Charm,* Webster's *Dirge.*

8. Moore, ed., *An Anthology of Pure Poetry,* pp. 17–18.

9. Alfred North Whitehead, *Adventures of Ideas* (New York, Cambridge University Press, 1933), p. 310.

tle cites as an instance of a poem "innocent of criticism of life" Wordsworth's lines *Written in March.*

> The Cock is crowing,
> The stream is flowing,
> The small birds twitter,
> The lake doth glitter,
> The green field sleeps in the sun;
> The oldest and youngest
> Are at work with the strongest;
> The cattle are grazing,
> Their heads never raising;
> There are forty feeding like one!

Unfortunately for my purposes, however, Pottle also includes as "pure
poetry" poetry which he calls "elliptical"—calling it pure "not because
it does not require the contemplation of doctrine or ideas, but because
the ideas, though present in the mind of the poet, have been squeezed
out of the poem and you are expected to supply them yourself as a
commentary." To my mind the difference between poetry that is really
"innocent of criticism of life" and poetry that requires the contemplation of ideas is so essential that the term "pure poetry" should be reserved for the poetry which Pottle terms "imagistic," [1] poetry that stays
as close as possible to what Northrop terms the "differentiated aesthetic
continuum," [2] avoiding as far as possible any connection with the theoretic—with abstract thought.

Obviously, since words by their very nature have conceptual value,
since every word, even the most concrete, involves to some extent an
abstraction, purity in poetry in the sense of complete aesthetic immediacy
with no theoretic content never exists. Every poem means something.
Middleton Murry reminds us "that there is already implicit in pure
poetry at the simplest level of perceptive experience a thought on nature
and on human life which is both pregnant and elusive." [3] Pottle finds

---

1. Pottle, *The Idiom of Poetry*, pp. 93–5, 99.

2. F. S. C. Northrop, *The Meeting of East and West, an Inquiry concerning World
Understanding* (New York, Macmillan, 1946), pp. 300–10. The distinction Northrop
makes between art which represents the differentiated aesthetic continuum and art which
embodies abstract concepts seems to bear directly on the discussion of "pure poetry."
Robert Penn Warren's essay, "Pure and Impure Poetry," *The Kenyon Review, 5*
(Spring, 1943), 228–54, seems to miss the point of the distinction between aesthetic and
theoretic values. Warren, evidently following Richards' distinction between synthetic and
exclusive poetry, uses the term "pure" of a poem which excludes "certain elements which
might qualify or contradict its original impulse" (p. 241) and ridicules the whole discussion of "pure poetry" as an attempt to locate poetry in an essence "at some particular
place in a poem, or in some particular element" (p. 246).

3. John Middleton Murry, "Pure Poetry," *Countries of the Mind*, p. 28. Murry regards
all poets as pure poets; in his opinion poetry stays pure whether it have much or little
thought value. He recognizes that the thought may be only "what we should ordinarily

it "as impossible to write a completely pure poem as it is to produce a completely pure chemical." [4] The very fact that no completely "pure" poetry exists indicates clearly that poetry does not reside in the sensuous alone. To isolate sensuous qualities and term them alone "aesthetic" is misleading; poetry requires always both sensuous and intellectual—a wholeness and completeness impossible in isolated qualities.

Insofar as poetry can ever convey only experience of the aesthetic component in the nature of things, however, it does so by naming things and their qualities. Things can be poetic in and of themselves and their associations: the most elementary poetry lies, as Rylands says, "in the mere names of natural objects." "The moon, the nightingale and the rose, orchards and gardens, amber and ivory, kings and queens, the months and stars and seasons, these are the current coin of poetry. . . . They are in themselves beautiful, poetic subjects, and possess secondary implications." [5] The poetry of things seems to be as close as poetry can come to being "pure" in the sense of being relatively devoid of abstract thought. John Crowe Ransom calls such poetry "physical poetry" and remarks that the art of poetry most frequently depends on "the faculty of presenting images so whole and clean that they resist the catalysis of thought." [6] Moore's anthology is good evidence that the poetry of things can be in its own way richly satisfying. Nor does it seem that the poetic value of things derives from their natural value as symbols. Santayana remarks that the poetry of Lucretius seems to be not "the poetry of a poet about things, but the poetry of things themselves." It is his opinion that the poetry comes not from the symbolic value of the things but from "their own movement and life." [7] Things seen whole and complete give one elemental poetry.

The poetry of things is perhaps a corrective to the tendency to identify poetry with language. Poetry inheres in the kind of language that symbolizes a concrete totality; it also inheres in things seen as concrete totalities. The danger of course is that one may come to think, as Addison and other writers of the eighteenth century thought, that poetry resides in the sublime or beautiful object. The theory of the poetic object is now rightly regarded as naive: a pretty object in and of itself no more makes poetry than do so many metaphors strung together. But it is easier to make poetry of an object than of an idea because even though the object as it appears in a poem is itself a mental

call a perception" and that a simple perception, "held in its uncontaminated wholeness, as the poet holds it for us, is at once ultimate and satisfying" (pp. 25, 28).

4. *The Idiom of Poetry*, p. 104.

5. George H. N. Rylands, *Words and Poetry* (New York, Payson & Clarke, 1938), pp. 55, 65.

6. "Poetry: A Note in Ontology," *The World's Body* (New York, Scribners, 1938), p. 118.

7. George Santayana, *Three Philosophical Poets, the Works of George Santayana* (Triton ed., New York, Scribners, 1936), 6, 24.

construct, it is easier to see an object in its fullness and wholeness than it is so to see an idea. The words the poet uses to describe the object inevitably introduce concepts, so that the very combination of words with things tends to produce a concrete totality.

The poetry of ideas—poetry that does not stop with things but conveys the life of the mind as well—obviously does not automatically give the poet concreteness to deal with as does poetry about things. The problem of the expression of ideas seems the real problem of great poetry. Putting abstract ideas into poetry results in versified prose—that much seems evident enough. Santayana, inquiring into the relationship of poetry to philosophy, comments that investigation and reasoning are eternally unpoetic; he finds the works of Epicurus or St. Thomas Aquinas or Kant to be "leafless forests." [8] But just as obviously poetry cannot exclude ideas and achieve any real totality. The greater the poet the more his vision includes an understanding of life and its values. Santayana has objected strenuously to the definition of "pure poetry" as a poetry that excludes ideas, pointing out that all the images and emotions that enter a cultivated mind are "saturated with theory." In his opinion "philosophy is a more intense sort of experience" than ordinary life just as music is a keener experience than ordinary noise. When a poet is "not mindless," philosophy inevitably appears in his poetry since it is part of his experience. "To object to theory in poetry would be like objecting to words there; for words, too, are symbols without the sensuous character of the things they stand for; and yet it is only by the net of new connections which words throw over things, in recalling them, that poetry arises at all." Poetry, says Santayana, is itself "a theoretic vision" of things. [9]

Yet Moore's antipathy to ideas in poetry is based on certain elements of truth. Ideas, by and large, are abstractions, remote from concrete reality; they are bare bones without flesh. The poet, according to Emerson, "like the electric rod, must reach from a point nearer the sky than all surrounding objects, down to the earth, and into the dark, wet soil, or neither is of use. The poet must not only converse with pure thought, but he must demonstrate it almost to the senses." [1] The trouble is that pure thought is exactly what cannot be so demonstrated. Pure thought lacks any concreteness; it has been abstracted out of the earth. Moreover, the more clearly isolated the idea the more it demands expression in language outside the poetic sphere. Ideas that are completely logical must be expressed in exactly defined, sharply differentiated terms.

Poetry in Santayana's definition is "a theoretic vision." The word

8. Santayana, p. 8.
9. P. 84.
1. Ralph Waldo Emerson, "Europe and European Books," *The Complete Works of Ralph Waldo Emerson,* ed. Edward Waldo Emerson (Boston, Houghton, Mifflin, 1903), *12,* 366.

"vision" seems significant. Poetic thought is intuitive rather than logical; it is a seeing rather than an analysis. Just as language in its poetic stage is undifferentiated, each word symbolizing a matrix of meaning that contains elements at once concrete and abstract, so ideas in their poetic stage are intuitions. This seems so self-evident that I state it as a truism: poetic thought is, if you like, a primitive kind of thinking; it is basic and primary, elemental and immediate.[2] The freshness of vision that one associates with great poetry results from the fact that in poetry the findings of the abstracting intelligence have been returned to the imagination which is once again prehending in individual wholes. The side of the mind that develops earliest—in the growth of civilization and in the growth of the individual—is active. None of which shames poetry. The subjects of poetry are not ideas that have been completely mastered and fully analyzed; poetry is not concerned with the ionization of heavy water or with the care and feeding of pigs. The subjects of poetry are the subjects that eternally defy complete analysis: life and death and love, the mysteries of creation and being before which wise men stand in wonder and humility.

Obviously, not all poetry is alike: some is closer to intuitive vision and some is closer to analytic thought. It seems possible to regard poetry and analytic prose as two extremes: lyric poetry and other kinds of poetry in which meanings tend to be ambiguous and indefinite rather than clear cut are close to the poetic pole; satiric poetry and other sorts which depend on disparities of meaning and sharp antitheses are well down the line toward prose meanings and prose techniques. There is no exact place on the line where poetry divides from prose: different sensibilities in different periods push the dividing point back and forth. The eighteenth century included in poetry much that the Romantic sensibility found prosaic; the "purist" movement of our own day seems determined to exclude all prose values as nearly as possible from poetry. The important point is that differences in form should rightly accompany—be expressive of—real differences in the kind of meaning being expressed. The more the idea to be conveyed is seen clearly isolated, the more the form must move toward prose; the less isolated and the more undifferentiated the idea, the more the form must be poetic. One would therefore expect to find in satiric poetry—and in didactic—much more literal statement of idea than one would expect to find in lyric poetry; the difference in poetic conception should lead to difference in expression.

Much recent criticism seems essentially an attempt to understand how ideas do fit into poetry. If I may oversimplify considerably, the possibilities seem to be three: the ideas may be stated and illustrated, the

2. See James on the relation between poetry and the activity of the mind, *Scepticism and Poetry*, chap. i. I should not need to point out that this view of poetry does not exclude from it the use of concepts developed by the analytic intelligence. The two sides of the mind constantly interact.

ideas may be implicit within the symbol, or the ideas may be stated as an integral part of the poet's total pattern. If one remembers that in poetic thought the idea has not yet separated out from the concrete form but is as yet one with it, it is easy to see where all three lie on the line between poetry and prose.

The first possibility—of ideas stated and illustrated—is obviously the closest to prose and is, to contemporary sensibility, most likely to seem prosaic. Dangerous as it is to make any sort of absolute statement—some poetry somewhere will always prove one wrong—I am tempted to say that when a literally stated idea appears for its own sake, then the values are prosaic. By this I mean that a prose paraphrase is never the poem: if it were, that "poem" would be more nearly prose than poetry. The essence of poetry seems to be the inseparability of the idea from the concrete form in which the idea appears; when the two are completely separable and not fused, prose results. In didactic poetry if the ideas are not subordinate to a total pattern that includes them but are the dominant element, illustrated and elaborated, the modern reader tends to wonder where the poetry is. Ransom calls such poetry Platonic poetry, objecting to it that poetry beginning with a thesis "does not contain real images but illustrations." [3] The early morality plays—with some exaggeration—seem to stand in the same relation to true drama that didactic poetry bears to poetry. In the greatest didactic poetry, of course, the poet's doctrine seems a point of departure rather than an end: *Paradise Lost* is to an extent didactic, but in Milton's attempt to justify the ways of God to man his doctrine is not so much illustrated by the poem as it is itself part of the concrete pattern of the poem.

Poetry that does without any sort of statement of idea is of course at the other extreme. Much poetry that seems at first glance to belong to the poetry of things is in reality poetry in which the idea is latent in the image. Murry quotes Goethe on the relation of the particular to the universal in poetry:

> There is a great difference between a poet who seeks the particular for the sake of the universal and one who seeks the universal in the particular. The former method breeds Allegory, where the particular is used only as an example, an instance, of the universal; but the latter is the true method of poetry. It expresses a particular without a thought of or a reference to the universal. But whoever has a living grasp of this particular grasps the universal with it, knowing it either not at all, or only long afterwards. [4]

In genuine poetic intuition the universal and the particular appear together; the concrete contains the universal.

3. *The World's Body*, p. 128.
4. Murry, "The Metaphysics of Poetry," *Countries of the Mind*, p. 54.

Most poetry of course lies between the two extremes. Frequently, as in Shakespeare's sonnet "That time of year thou mayst in me behold," the poet presents a number of images, each of which holds his idea in suspense, leading finally to a literal statement of idea. The movement of the thought which proceeds from images which contain the idea to the clearly stated idea seems right: when the idea precipitates out from the image, the poem ends. The best recent criticism grapples intensively with the nature of poetry that does not yield to prose purposes and does not sacrifice meaning. The point that Wimsatt's theory of the "concrete universal," Ransom's of "texture and structure," and Tate's of "tension" in poetry [5] seem, for example, to have in common is this attempt to define the nature of poetry that is at once intellectually and aesthetically satisfying. The only general agreement at present seems to be that poetry serves essentially to create whole experiences, to restore the unity of experience that the analytic reason is forever destroying. Wimsatt insists on the complication and complexity of the individual work of art; [6] Ransom believes that "the poet must find his way back to those whole states of mind in which the world is originally experienced, and from which every pure intellectual achievement had to take its start"; [7] Tate regards poetry as "complete knowledge." [8] I am even tempted to include "irony" in the sense in which Richards and Brooks use it as another new name for this wholeness of experience.[9] Susanne Langer insists that artistic symbols "are untranslatable; their sense is bound to the particular form which it has taken." Even in poetry in which the material is verbal the real import, Langer says, "is not the literal assertion made in the words, but *the way the assertion is made.*" The significance of a poem "is purely implicit in the poem as a totality." "The poem as a whole is the symbol the poet has created to stand for his intuition the more genuinely poetic the intuition, the more the idea is one with the concrete form.

Language and poetry alike point to the central importance of poetic imagery. Inherently poetic language is undifferentiated language, lan-

5. W. K. Wimsatt, "The Structure of the 'Concrete Universal' in Literature," *PMLA,* 62 (March, 1947), 262–80; Ransom, *The New Criticism,* pp. 91–4, 280; Allen Tate, "Tension in Poetry," *Reason in Madness* (New York, Putnam's, 1941), pp. 62–81.

6. Wimsatt, pp. 272, 275–6.

7. John Crowe Ransom, "The Making of a Modern: The Poetry of George Marion O'Donnell," *The Southern Review, 1* (Spring, 1936), 872.

8. Allen Tate, "Literature as Knowledge: Comment and Comparison," *The Southern Review, 6* (1940–41), 656.

9. Ivor A. Richards, *Principles of Literary Criticism* (New York, Harcourt, Brace, 1930), 248–51. Richards finds the value of all the arts in the equilibrium—the balance and reconciliation—of opposed impulses. Irony in his view tests the presence of such equilibrium. Cleanth Brooks, "Irony and 'Ironic' Poetry," *College English, 9* (February, 1948), 231–7, similarly makes "Invulnerability to irony . . . the stability of a context in which the internal pressures balance and mutually support each other."

1. *Philosophy in a New Key,* pp. 261–2.

guage in which concrete and theoretic are held in one whole. Similarly ideas in their poetic stage are intuitive, primary apprehensions in which the concrete and the abstract are still a unit. Undifferentiated language and intuitive thought both involve the image as the central core of the vision of the wholeness of things. The "proper function and excellence" of poetry, as Murry says, is "to pursue its rhythmic progress through an identity of image and idea." [2] Eliminate the imagery and you eliminate both poetry and poem—both aesthetic power and meaning.

The two essentials of imagery upon which critics seem agreed are some form of sensory appeal and some form of nonliteralness, or, to use a less awkward expression, obliqueness.[3] Much confusion has been created by the fact that different kinds of images present different degrees of the two qualities. Literal imagery has sensory appeal but no obliqueness; figurative imagery has obliqueness and varying degrees of sensory appeal.[4] Various writers have objected to the tendency to identify imagery solely with sensory appeals,[5] Richards in particular objecting to the assumption "that a figure of speech, an image, or imaginative comparison, must have something to do with the presence of images" in the sense of an image as "a copy or revival of a sense-perception of some sort." "We cannot too firmly recognize," says Richards, "that how a figure of speech works has nothing necessarily to do with how any images, as copies or duplicates of sense perceptions, may, for reader or writer, be backing up his words." [6] The parallel tendency to identify imagery solely with the process of analogy has been less clearly recognized as mistaken. Richards is right, of course, in thinking that language may be at once metaphoric and abstract, without image-making power.[7] But it seems unnecessarily confusing to use the term "imagery" for such formations.[8] Just as most students of imagery do not attempt to deal with purely literal imagery, which lacks obliqueness, so most do

2. "Reason and Criticism," *Countries of the Mind*, p. 38.

3. See René Wellek and Austin Warren, "Image, Metaphor, Symbol, Myth," *Theory of Literature* (New York, Harcourt, Brace, 1949), pp. 190–4.

4. In general usage an image may be simply "a representation of something to the mind by speech or writing; a vivid or graphic description" and imagery the "descriptive representation of ideas." In rhetorical usage an image is "a simile, metaphor, or figure of speech" and imagery is "the use of rhetorical images." *OED.* Literal imagery is then anything described without figures of speech in such a way as to appeal to the mind through the senses. See the unsigned article on imagery, *Dictionary of World Literature*, ed. Joseph T. Shipley (New York, Philosophical Library, 1943), p. 311.

5. See especially Fogle, *The Imagery of Keats and Shelley*, pp. 4–10. See also Caroline F. E. Spurgeon, *Shakespeare's Imagery and What It Tells Us* (New York, Macmillan, 1935), p. 5.

6. *The Philosophy of Rhetoric*, p. 98.

7. P. 129.

8. See the discussion of Johnson's imagery in W. K. Wimsatt, *The Prose Style of Samuel Johnson* (New Haven, Yale University Press, 1941), 65. Wimsatt agrees with Spurgeon that imagery should mean something at once non-literal and pictorial, and finds that Johnson's writing can be said to contain imagery only in the sense of "simply non-literal expression."

not attempt to deal with metaphoric constructions that lack concreteness. Most poetic figures do work in connection with sensory images; when the figure fails even faintly to stir an imaginative picture (not necessarily visual), aesthetic power is gone.

Perhaps in consequence of this overreaction against the tendency to identify imagery with sensory appeal, most recent students of imagery have focused on the metaphor to the neglect of the symbol. The symbol has of all figurative images the most concrete body and the least obliqueness. Coleridge recognized its importance, complaining,

> It is among the miseries of the present age that it recognizes no *medium* between literal and metaphorical. Faith is either to be buried in the dead letter, or its name and honors usurped by a counterfeit product of the mechanical understanding, which in the blindness of self-complacency confounds symbols with allegories. Now an allegory is but a translation of abstract notions into a picture-language, which is itself nothing but an abstraction from objects of the senses; the principal being more worthless even than its phantom proxy, both alike unsubstantial, and the former shapeless to boot. On the other hand a symbol . . . is characterized by a translucence of the special in the individual, or of the general in the special, or of the universal in the general; above all by the translucence of the eternal through and in the temporal.[9]

The symbol looks literal and can be read literally. But on the line of which poetry and prose are the two extremes the symbol is at the poetic pole. It makes no actual comparison; the universal is seen *in* the particular. In its simultaneous presentation and representation it presents layers of meaning that open out indefinitely; in the blinding of Gloucester and the madness of Lear, in the white whale, in Dante's rose, the concrete object or action embodies additional nonliteral meanings.

Moreover, as Wimsatt has pointed out,

> The best story poems may be analyzed . . . as metaphors without expressed tenors, as symbols which speak for themselves. "La Belle Dame Sans Merci" . . . is about a knight, . . . and about a faery lady with wild, wild eyes. At a more abstract level, it is about the loss of self in the mysterious lure of beauty—whether woman, poetry, or poppy. It sings the irretrievable departure from practical normality (the squirrel's granary is full), the wan isolation after ecstasy. . . . A good story poem is like a stone thrown into a pond, into our minds, where ever widening concentric circles of meaning go out—and this because of the structure of the story.[1]

9. Samuel Taylor Coleridge, *The Statesman's Manual, the Complete Works of Samuel Taylor Coleridge,* ed. W. G. T. Shedd (New York, Harper, 1884), *1,* 437.

1. Wimsatt, "The Structure of the 'Concrete Universal,'" *PMLA, 62* (March, 1947), 275.

Wordsworth's *Goody Blake and Harry Gill* seems to have been intended as such a story poem. Wordsworth wished "to draw attention to the truth that the power of the human imagination is sufficient to produce such changes even in our physical nature as might almost appear miraculous."[2] Unfortunately there is no adequate symbol in the poem for the power of the imagination comparable to the faery lady as a symbol of beauty, and the poem—at least for this reader—remains a curious literal anecdote that fails to spread concentric circles of meaning. But the fact remains that the completely literal poem may be literal only on the surface, that Wordsworth's daffodils are daffodils and something more, and that Wordsworth constantly compels one to recognize the symbolic power of the seemingly literal.

The best metaphors are difficult to distinguish from symbols. Warren finds the only important difference to be "the recurrence and persistence of the 'symbol.'"[3] But in the metaphor the concrete basis has ceased to be actual; it is only suggested. In *The River Duddon* sonnets Wordsworth writes at once of actual river, of his own life, of the life stream of mankind; there is no escaping the presence of the actual river. In the *Ecclesiastical Sonnets* Wordsworth employs the river as a recurrent metaphor but there is no actual river. From the actual river the idea of a current or stream flowing and developing through time has been abstracted out and applied to the growth and development of the church. Metaphor always involves this abstraction of certain qualities from one object or concept and their application to another. To follow the definition of W. Bedell Stanford, metaphor is "the process and result of using a term (X) normally signifying an object or concept (A) in such a context that it must refer to another object or concept (B) which is distinct enough in characteristics from A to ensure that in the composite idea formed by the syntheses of the concepts A and B and now symbolized in the word X, the factors A and B retain their conceptual independence even while they merge in the unity symbolized by X."[4]

But while abstraction has taken place, in good metaphor this new unity is less an exact and easily definable meaning than an evocative cluster which yields indefinite layers of meaning. Like the primary symbol true metaphor is creative; it seems the mind's process for discovery. "Genuine new ideas," says Susanne Langer, ". . . usually have to break in upon the mind through some great and bewildering metaphor."[5] The metaphor appears less a conscious abstraction of a quality

---

2. "Preface to the Second Edition of Several of the Foregoing Poems, Published, with an Additional Volume, under the Title of 'Lyrical Ballads,'" *PW, 2,* 401, n. 2. Hereafter this will be referred to as "Preface to the Lyrical Ballads."

3. Wellek and Warren, *Theory of Literature,* pp. 193–4.

4. *Greek Metaphor: Studies in Theory and Practice* (Oxford, Basil Blackwell, 1936), p. 101.

5. *Philosophy in a New Key,* p. 201.

from one object by which to illuminate the same quality in a second than a seeing of the two things together, less a joining of things previously separate than a togetherness of things which to the analytic consciousness appear disparate.

The question of the nature of metaphor thus seems perilously allied to the nature of thought and the development of consciousness. Murry's statement that if one thinks long enough about metaphor one approaches the borderline of sanity is profoundly true.[6] Metaphor is a process of the mind; it is, as Murry says, "almost a mode of apprehension." [7] In metaphor and symbol alike, the direct and imaginative side of the mind prehends in individual wholes.[8] For this reason much of the contemporary discussion of metaphor seems to me based on serious misconceptions about the nature of metaphor. Too many writers go on the assumption that in metaphor separate things have been mechanically joined, failing to perceive that an organic unity may have been created.[9]

Richards' distinction between tenor and vehicle—the tenor the poet's subject and the vehicle the image the poet uses to speak of the subject—consequently seems to me misleading. Richards thinks that "talk about the identification or fusion that a metaphor effects is nearly always misleading and pernicious. In general, there are few metaphors in which disparities between tenor and vehicle are not as much operative as the similarities." [1] I should maintain that the poetic metaphor either originates in a fusion or restores a unity, and that the more nearly the disparities become obvious the more the metaphor is moving away from symbol toward simile. The image of Cleopatra's barge seems a case in point:

> The barge she sat in, like a burnish'd throne,
> Burn'd on the water.[2]

Assuredly no one thinks distinctly of fire. *Burn'd* conveys as no literal word could the sheer glory of it—carrying at the same time unmistakably the overtones of passion. The glow and warmth and ecstasy of Cleopatra herself seem to lie behind the description of her barge. The simile *like a burnish'd throne,* exactly because the two elements have become separate and distinct, lacks the indefinite layers of meaning that give *burn'd* its power.

Because metaphor, like symbol, is not an artificial joining but an organic birth, a good deal of the contemporary argument concerning

6. "Metaphor," *Countries of the Mind,* p. 1.
7. *The Problem of Style* (New York, Oxford University Press, 1922), p. 13.
8. See above, p. 3.
9. This organic unity is of course accessible to analysis. The discursive intellect analyzes what the imagination brings together.
1. *The Philosophy of Rhetoric,* p. 127.
2. *The Tragedy of Antony and Cleopatra,* II, ii, 199–200.

the logical or emotional nature of the ground connecting the so-called tenor and vehicle seems likewise misleading.[3] Certainly since the metaphor enables the poet to say what he wishes to say, the ground of the metaphor can seldom be completely emotional. Equally certainly, if the ground were completely logical the result would not be a metaphor. Ransom observes, "The moment the metaphor is perfectly subdued to its logical function in the meaning it ceases to be a metaphor." [4] Father Brown seems right in saying that the idea "seeks expression in terms adequate not merely to the intellectual concept, but to one's emotional possession of it." He finds that the writer using metaphor does not primarily aim at "clearness of logical statement" but rather desires expression that in its vigor and intensity will "bear some resemblance and proportion to the inner frame of mind." [5] In the metaphor as in the symbol, idea, emotion, and image fuse: the richness of the metaphor of Cleopatra's barge that burned on the water comes from the indefinite emotional overtones that accompany the indefinite core of meaning. The ground of such a metaphor is both emotional and logical.

The function of metaphor seems consequently to be on a small scale very much like the function of poetry itself. The poem as a whole is the symbol the poet creates to stand for his intuition or vision; the metaphor is the symbol of smaller intuitions. It is a way of creating meaning, of expressing what otherwise cannot be said. Richards in objecting to the eighteenth-century view that it is tenor alone that matters has remarked that "vehicle and tenor in co-operation give a meaning of more varied powers than can be ascribed to either." [6] In spite of the fact that here as elsewhere Richards seems to think of the metaphor more as a joining than as a birth, his point that the meaning of the whole metaphor is something that no part of it means alone is a good one. Murry objects to "the conception that the metaphor is in any useful sense of the word an ornament," pointing out that "for most of the things whose quality a writer wishes to convey there are no precise epithets, simply because he is engaged in discovering their qualities." [7]

3. Rosemond Tuve, "Imagery and Logic: Ramus and Metaphysical Poets," *Journal of the History of Ideas, 3* (October, 1942), 376, insists that "the distinguishing feature of an image, by reference to which it may be compared with others, and its origin conjectured, is the *logical basis* upon which the poet has perceived comparableness." C. W. Valentine, "The Function of Images in the Appreciation of Poetry," *The British Journal of Psychology, 14* (October, 1923), 181, argues that the most truly poetic bond "is the bond of feeling rather than of similarity." Max Rieser, "Analysis of the Poetic Simile," *The Journal of Philosophy, 37* (April, 1940), 216, defines an image as "an emotional analogy consisting of a process wherein two objects possessing a similar emotional value for human feeling or, more exactly, two kindred emotional halos are compared within the sensibility."
4. *The New Criticism*, p. 259.
5. Stephen J. Brown, *The World of Imagery: Metaphor and Kindred Imagery* (London, Kegan Paul, Trench, Trubner, 1927), p. 56.
6. *The Philosophy of Rhetoric*, p. 100.
7. *The Problem of Style*, p. 83.

"All metaphor and simile," says Murry in his penetrating essay on metaphor, "can be described as the analogy by which the human mind explores the universe of quality and charts the non-measurable world." [8]

Simile, as Buck argued,[9] is a step closer to literal speech, involving still more abstraction than the metaphor. The cluster of meaning that appears in primary perception has in simile divided into distinct parts; clarity and exactness are gained, but at the loss of richness. The tenor-vehicle distinction which splits metaphor apart serves admirably when one is concerned with simile. Obviously in the simile fusion never occurs, but the two terms remain equivalent. In

> The stroke of death is as a lover's pinch,
> Which hurts, and is desir'd,[1]

the effect depends, as James observes,[2] upon the violence of the contrast. Cleopatra's

> Dost thou not see my baby at my breast,
> That sucks the nurse asleep? [3]

demonstrates that in metaphor, even when disparity is extreme, vehicle and tenor are still seen simultaneously. What seems evident is that the closer the metaphor is to symbol, the more its parts will remain together; the nearer the metaphor is to simile, the more its parts will separate.

In imagery as in language and poetry there are degrees of wholeness. One can discover a progression from the concrete totality of primary perception to the divided elements of analytic thought. The "inseparable conglomerations" give way to combinable short elements. Poetry is the kind of expression symbolizing perceptions that are still wholes, but different sensibilities in different periods are excited or satisfied by different degrees of wholeness. Just as some poetry is closer to the rational, analytic mode of thought than to the intuitive mode, some images are more nearly logical than others.[4] As logical clarity increases poetic wholeness will tend to diminish. Therefore any discussion of the function of imagery in the abstract is likely to be misleading. Obviously the exact function of the image varies from poem to poem, from writer to writer, from period to period. But whether the poem be a metaphysical one in which the metaphor serves as logical structure, or an Augustan

---

8. In *Countries of the Mind*, p. 9.
9. *The Metaphor*, pp. 36–40.
1. *The Tragedy of Antony and Cleopatra*, v, ii, 297–8.
2. *Scepticism and Poetry*, p. 106.
3. v, ii, 311–12.
4. Louis MacNeice, *Modern Poetry, a Personal Essay* ([New York], Oxford University Press, 1938), p. 92, divides imagery similarly into the cerebral which originates in reason and the emotional or physical or intuitive which comes from the senses or the unconscious. "Cerebral imagery" would to my mind approach the prose pole; intuitive, the poetic.

one in which the image is used to illustrate a stated idea, or a Romantic one in which, as Lewis says, the image "is a mode of exploring reality," [5] every image seems in some degree to serve to convey thought-emotion imaginatively.

All three words of the foregoing phrase are essential: the image creates meaning, but it inevitably conveys not only meaning but the poet's emotion and his imaginative apprehension as well. Father Brown considers that the metaphor, "besides enriching our resources for the expression of thought, introduces into language the elements of *con-creteness, of feeling, and of aesthetic pleasure.*" [6] Murry, to whom I owe the term "thought-emotion," in his study of Keats' *On First Look-ing into Chapman's Homer* shows that Keats seems to have accumulated a series of images which could "be assimilated into the main process of his thought and act as surrogates for it. And the condition of this as-similation is an emotional and qualitative correspondence." [7] Those critics who stress only the intellectual function of imagery [8] appear to have been misled by the importance of abstract thought in contem-porary civilization into forgetting that poetry and metaphor alike repre-sent a different mode of apprehension, less abstract and intellectual, more aesthetic and more total. The distinguishing feature of this thinking is its wholeness—logical relation, emotion, and concrete perception merg-ing inextricably so that the poet finds a way of giving his thought at once concrete body, imaginative life, and emotional warmth.

Imagery, then, is the central core of both language and poetry. In it the sensuous, the emotional, and the intellectual merge, and the vision of life is whole. It seems reasonable to suppose, therefore, that a poet's genius will appear most clearly in the figurative images that he creates to convey his meaning, that study of a poet's imagery will reveal the poet's basic intuitions concerning reality. In search of Wordsworth's imagina-tive vision of life let us turn to Wordsworth's poetry.

5. *The Poetic Image*, p. 58.

6. *The World of Imagery*, p. 93. The concreteness would seem to me to be part of the aesthetic pleasure. See also Stanford, *Greek Metaphor*, p. 45. Stanford does not specifi-cally discuss the function of metaphor but finds the chief sources of delight in it to be its appeal to the intellect, to the senses and the imagination, and to the emotions.

7. John Middleton Murry, *Studies in Keats New and Old* (2d ed., London, Oxford University Press, 1939), pp. 19–33. See also the discussion of this poem in Wimsatt, "The Structure of the 'Concrete Universal,'" *PMLA, 62* (March, 1947), 274. Wimsatt regards the whole poem as a metaphor of which the real subject is "a certain kind of thrill in discovering, for which there is no name and no other description."

8. Richard Blackmur in "Notes on Four Categories in Criticism," *The Sewanee Review, 54* (1946), 580–1, thinks that figures of speech "when not merely ornamental, have as their commonest function to clarify the workings of the images which are their chief elements: they combine the concrete image present in the field of the given work with some abstraction of another image." Ruth Herschberger in "The Structure of Meta-phor," *Kenyon Review, 5* (Summer, 1943), 433, similarly regards metaphor as "fun-damentally an expository and . . . economic prose usage." See also Rosemond Tuve, *Elizabethan and Metaphysical Imagery* (Chicago, University of Chicago Press, 1947), Pt. II.

II

All Things Blending into One

INDIVIDUAL metaphors and similes in Wordsworth's poetry, considered either in isolation or within the context of single poems, are so subordinate in nature, so unobtrusive in effect, as at first to be disappointing. The *Lyrical Ballads* are starkly bare: Wordsworth was sloughing off all ornament, presenting the thing in itself. They are *naked* poems. The *Poems* of 1807 are less bare; Helen Darbishire speaks of their "fuller melodies and richer imagery." [1] By the time of *The Excursion,* as is well known, the bare style had given way to one that is in many ways classical.[2] In the late poetry, imagery at times seems to be simply ornament. But taking his poetry in bulk and considering particularly the poetry of the great decade, it seems fair to say that the characteristics of the individual metaphor or simile are at first sight negative. The single metaphor or simile is not an organizing image, it is not complex, it is not startling.

Let us look, for example, at the central passage of "There was a Boy" which includes the lines that Coleridge said he should have recognized anywhere; had he met "these lines running wild in the deserts of Arabia," he should "have instantly screamed out 'Wordsworth!' " [3]

> And, when there came a pause
> Of silence such as baffled his best skill:
> Then sometimes, in that silence, while he hung
> Listening, a gentle shock of mild surprise
> Has carried far into his heart the voice
> Of mountain-torrents; or the visible scene
> Would enter unawares into his mind
> With all its solemn imagery, its rocks,
> Its woods, and that uncertain heaven received
> Into the bosom of the steady lake.[4]

The unobtrusive nature of the imagery is characteristic of Wordsworth. Outside of a few sonnets, I can think of no poem which is de-

1. "Introduction," *Wordsworth: Poems in Two Volumes, 1807,* ed. Helen Darbishire (Oxford, Clarendon Press, 1914), p. lii.
2. See especially Judson S. Lyon, "The Style of *The Excursion,*" *The Excursion, A Study* (New Haven, Yale University Press, 1950), chap. v.
3. Letter to Wordsworth, December 10, 1798, quoted in Christopher Wordsworth, *Memoirs of William Wordsworth* (London, Moxon, 1851), I, 137.
4. Ll. 16–25.

veloped by means of an extended metaphor; metaphor rarely if ever controls structure. That it does not by no means results in imagery which is decorative. The figures here—the boy *hung* listening, *far into* his heart, the *voice* of mountain torrents—are certainly not decorative; they are, as Wordsworth would put it, "a constituent part and power or function in the thought." [5] The thought deals with the way feelings— here of surprise—impress images upon the mind.[6] The boy's mind is viewed spatially and the images of sound and sight are endowed with activity in order to convey the thought.

Even in the *Ode on Intimations of Immortality* where light metaphors are recurrent, the metaphors do not form the structure or framework on which the poem is built. The individual metaphors contribute to our awareness of light as a symbol of the life of the spirit and are essential to the development of the adult-child pattern. But the vehicle is not held constant; "that immortal sea / Which brought us hither," "that imperial palace whence he [the child] came" are other metaphors that contribute to total meaning. Some of the sonnets, however, do have a sustained, controlling metaphor. London and Venice are both made living persons; [7] liberty speaks through the voices of sea and mountain flood.[8] *Composed upon Westminster Bridge, Sept. 3, 1802,* in which the personification of London becomes obvious only in the last line, is more characteristic of Wordsworth's methods than is the sonnet on Venice in which the image of a woman controls the entire poem. It is not characteristic of Wordsworth to sustain a metaphor long or to use a metaphor or simile as an organizing device.

Nor are the individual images complex. If it seems unfair to consider only "There was a Boy," admittedly one of the simplest of the *Poems of the Imagination,*[9] take the first two stanzas of *Resolution and Independence:*

> There was a roaring in the wind all night;
> The rain came heavily and fell in floods;
> But now the sun is rising calm and bright;
> The birds are singing in the distant woods;
> Over his own sweet voice the Stock-dove broods;

5. See below, p. 130.

6. Wordsworth began his *Poems of the Imagination* "with one of the earliest processes of Nature in the development of this faculty. Guided by one of my own primary consciousnesses, I have presented a commutation and transfer of internal feelings, co-operating with external accidents, to plant, for immortality, images of sound and sight, in the celestial soil of the Imagination." "Preface to the Edition of 1815," *PW, 2,* 440, n. 2.

7. *Composed upon Westminster Bridge, Sept. 3, 1802* and *On the Extinction of the Venetian Republic.*

8. *Thought of a Briton on the Subjugation of Switzerland.*

9. See Wordsworth's comment, "Preface to the Edition of 1815," *PW, 2,* 440, n. 2, text of 1815–36.

The Jay makes answer as the Magpie chatters;
And all the air is filled with pleasant noise of waters.

All things that love the sun are out of doors;
The sky rejoices in the morning's birth;
The grass is bright with rain-drops;—on the moors
The hare is running races in her mirth;
And with her feet she from the plashy earth
Raises a mist; that, glittering in the sun,
Runs with her all the way, wherever she doth run.

Even the comparison later in the poem of the old man to the stone and the stone to a seabeast, which Wordsworth cited as an example of the modifying power of images upon each other, can hardly be called complex. Probably the most complex image in the entire body of Wordsworth's poetry appears in the fifth stanza of the *Intimations* ode, a passage that has been fully discussed by Cleanth Brooks.[1]
[Nor are the individual images startling. What Wordsworth wanted was "a gentle shock of mild surprise.] Like all poets he observed "affinities / In objects where no brotherhood exists / To passive minds," [2] but such affinities never extended to relationships between compasses and lovers or a fleabite and the satisfaction of love. Since Wordsworth distinguished between affinities that are merely playful and those that are essentially true, one would expect to find unusual vehicles in his poems of fancy if anywhere.[In Wordsworth's opinion, when the nature of things does not sustain the combination made in an image, the image is the work of the fancy.] But one looks in vain for any figure in which there is really startling disparity between the terms. Falling leaves and parachutes; clouds and helmets; girls and lilies, fawns, clouds; daisy and nun, maiden, queen, starveling, Cyclops, silver shield, and star; bone-house and garden [3]—the disparity is never so great that the image must be developed at length to explain the connection. Bone-house and garden is as violent a yoking as Wordsworth makes.

Maynard Mack has very properly observed that in images where there is great disparity between tenor and vehicle—as in Donne's lovers and compasses—the power of the comparison is limited, the small area of likeness leaving no room in which the image can expand.[4] Images that

1. See "Wordsworth and the Paradox of the Imagination," *The Well Wrought Urn* (New York, Reynal & Hitchcock, 1947), pp. 119–23.
2. *The Prelude*, II, 384–6.
3. *The Kitten and Falling Leaves,* l. 16; *Song for the Wandering Jew,* l. 7; *The Seven Sisters or the Solitude of Binnorie,* ll. 5, 26, 46; *To the Daisy* (With little here); *To a Sexton,* stanza 3.
4. " 'Wit and Poetry and Pope': Some Observations on His Imagery," in *Pope and His Contemporaries: Essays Presented to George Sherburn,* ed. J. L. Clifford and L. A. Landa (Oxford, Clarendon Press, 1949), pp. 23–4.

are nourished by normal and traditional associations do not need to be developed at length, having, as Mack puts it, reserve power. Truly imaginative images, according to Wordsworth, are sustained by the nature of things. "When the Imagination frames a comparison, if it does not strike on the first presentation, a sense of the truth of the likeness, from the moment that it is perceived, grows—and continues to grow—upon the mind; the resemblance depending less upon outline of form and feature, than upon expression and effect; less upon casual and outstanding, than upon inherent and internal, properties." [5] In such images the connecting link between the two terms of the image is not mere Hartleian association or contiguity in time or space. Some such associations are made, of course,[6] but they are not to be confused with images where the relationship depends on inherent and internal properties. The reader has only to recall such lines as

> The intellectual power, through words and things,
> Went sounding on, a dim and perilous way!

> The marble index of a mind for ever
> Voyaging through strange seas of Thought, alone,

> The still, sad music of humanity.

> thy mind
> Shall be a mansion for all lovely forms.[7]

Within the poem, although a single image does not determine structure, the separate images do develop a pattern about the central image. The poet wandered lonely as a cloud; the daffodils were a crowd, a host, continuous as the stars in the milky way, a jocund company.[8] In *Nutting* the *virgin* scene that promises a *banquet* is *ravaged* and left *mutilated*. In "She was a Phantom of delight" the poet develops in turn the attractiveness of the woman on slight acquaintance, on better knowledge, and on complete knowledge. The central image, the woman, is developed by numerous brief images which keep a certain pattern. At first she *gleams,* and except for the dusky hair all the images are bright and gay and dancing. Then, better known, she is

> A Creature not too bright or good
> For human nature's daily food;

5. "Preface to the Edition of 1815," *PW, 2,* 441.
6. See for example *Michael,* ll. 62 ff.; *The Two April Mornings,* ll. 21 ff.; *The Prelude,* I, 597 ff.; *The Old Cumberland Beggar,* ll. 87 ff.
7. *The Excursion,* III, 700-1, cf. *The Borderers,* l. 1775; *The Prelude,* III, 62-3; *Tintern Abbey,* l. 91; *Tintern Abbey,* ll. 139-40.
8. "I wandered lonely as a cloud."

and finally, her inmost nature is

> a Spirit still, and bright
> With something of angelic light.

Since it is not my intention to present a series of analyses of separate poems, I cannot develop this point more fully here. Throughout my discussion of Wordsworth's major symbols, however, the reader will find a certain number of poems fully enough discussed to develop this point more adequately.[9]

The real strength and power of Wordsworth's metaphors and similes emerges, however, not from any single image or any single poem but from the entire body of his poetry, for his images are not only supported by the nature of things: they are supported by each other so that every image has behind it the reserve strength of the entire body of Wordsworth's poetry. Wordsworth did not anticipate being known through a single poem or a few poems. In his preface to the 1814 edition of *The Excursion* he wrote that the attentive reader would find his minor pieces "to have such connection with the main Work as may give them claim to be likened to the little cells, oratories, and sepulchral recesses" ordinarily accompanying a Gothic church. The present-day critic who demands that each poem be read without reference to the rest of the author's work wishes, if I may continue Wordsworth's metaphor, to contemplate one cell while ignoring the cathedral. Throughout Wordsworth's poetry human beings are steadily seen in terms of natural objects—the reader has only to recall "Three years she grew in sun and shower," *Lucy Gray,* and "She was a Phantom of delight"—natural objects are seen in terms of other natural objects, the inanimate in terms of the animate and also in terms of human beings. A great crosscurrent of imagery results wherein the human is natural and the natural is alive. "Three years she grew in sun and shower," *Nutting,* and *The Simplon Pass* express this interrelationship within the limits of single poems; it appears most fully, however, not in any one poem but in the steady interplay of images. The first twenty lines of *The Prelude* yield, by way of illustration, the breeze half conscious of the joy it brings, the cloud guide, the poet "Free as a bird." No other crosscurrent of imagery is so strong or so consistently maintained as this one: early and late, human is natural and natural is alive. In 1842 comes the sonnet

> *A Poet!*—He hath put his heart to school,
> Nor dares to move unpropped upon the staff
> Which Art hath lodged within his hand—must laugh
> By precept only, and shed tears by rule.

9. See especially my discussions of *Tintern Abbey,* the *Intimations* ode, and *Michael,* below, pp. 39–42, 67–9, 56–7.

Thy Art be Nature; the live current quaff,
And let the groveller sip his stagnant pool,
In fear that else, when Critics grave and cool
Have killed him, Scorn should write his epitaph.
How does the Meadow-flower its bloom unfold?
Because the lovely little flower is free
Down to its root, and, in that freedom, bold;
And so the grandeur of the Forest-tree
Comes not by casting in a formal mould,
But from its *own* divine vitality.[1]

Other, lesser crosscurrents run fairly steadily throughout Wordsworth's poetry. Light appears in terms of sound and sound in terms of
light and both in terms of water.[2] So far as is consistent with "a gentle
shock of mild surprise," everything appears in terms of everything else
and nothing is seen isolated. Attributes of one object are attributed
to another so that the images make the "two objects unite and coalesce
in a just comparison." [3] For example, in a poem on the robin the weather
is "unruffled"; [4] the broom expects the butterfly to find in its blossoms
"wings lovely as his own." [5] While the miller and the two girls dance,
"Each leaf, that and this, his neighbour will kiss." [6] Coleridge's

O! the one Life within us and abroad,
Which meets all motion and becomes its soul,
A light in sound, a sound-like power in light,
Rhythm in all thought, and joyance everywhere— [7]

1. See also *To the Clouds,* where the clouds are an army, winged hosts, children of the
sea, like aerial birds, pilgrims in a caravan coming from a fount of life invisible. They are
welcome
> to my soul that owns in them,
> And in the bosom of the firmament
> O'er which they move, wherein they are contained,
> A type of her capacious self and all
> Her restless progeny.
>   Ll. 49–53
2. For example see "Three years she grew in sun and shower," ll. 29–30,
> And beauty born of murmuring sound
> Shall pass into her face;
Airey-Force Valley, l. 14, where the ash in the breeze makes "A soft eye-music of slow-
waving boughs"; *Power of Music,* l. 14, where the fiddler is a "centre of light"; *The
Prelude,* xiv, 73, where the voices of the abyss issue "forth to silent light"; *The Prelude,*
ii, 204 ff., where in writing of the power of sound Wordsworth speaks of drinking the
visionary power; *The Prelude,* iv, 328, "drenched in empyrean light"; and *On the Power
of Sound,* ll. 47–50, 209.
3. "Preface to the Edition of 1815," *PW, 2,* 438.
4. *The Redbreast,* l. 62.
5. *The Oak and the Broom,* l. 84.
6. *Stray Pleasures,* l. 34.
7. *The Eolian Harp,* ll. 26–9.

perfectly describes not only Wordsworth's metaphysics but the cumula-
tive effect of Wordsworth's metaphors and similes. Wordsworth himself at least three times in *The Prelude* describes the unity of all things.[8]
Whether he terms it "one life" or the "workings of one mind" or "One
galaxy of life and joy," [9] the point is the same. All things blend into
one,[1] and metaphor and simile are the means to the blending, the connecting tissue that holds human and natural together in a unity that is
divine.

All things blend into one in still another fashion, however. When one
has seen that the single image is unobtrusive, that images interact to
support each other across the entire body of Wordsworth's poetry, one
has still only begun to know how to read Wordsworth. His most significant imagery is often apparently literal: usually its significance is
made explicit, as it is in *The Simplon Pass* where brook and road and
winds and crags become the

> workings of one mind, the features
> Of the same face, blossoms upon one tree,
> Characters of the great Apocalypse;
> The types and symbols of Eternity,
> Of first, and last, and midst, and without end.[2]

But such patterns are not always so explicit. In our original illustration
from "There was a Boy" there is, I think, the latent suggestion that the
visible scene enters unaware into the boy's mind very much as the uncertain heaven is received into the bosom of the lake. Wimsatt has already called attention to the fact that in Romantic nature imagery in
general, tenor and vehicle tend to draw from the same material: the
interest lies not in disparity but in the pattern within "the multiform
sensuous picture." [3] This comment seems to me to point to the most
profitable area for study within Wordsworth—the seemingly literal
that is serving as vehicle. "A poet's heart and intellect should be *combined*," wrote Coleridge, "intimately combined and unified with the
great appearances of nature." [4] Wordsworth's heart and intellect were so
intimately combined with the great appearances of nature that his
unique vision can be discovered most clearly not from the study of
separate poems but from the study of his recurrent symbols.[5]

8. II, A, 415–34; VI, 624–40; VIII, A, 623–39.
9. II, A, 430; VI, 636; VIII, A, 630.
1. See *Composed in Roslin Chapel during a Storm*, l. 14.
2. Ll. 16–20.
3. W. K. Wimsatt, "The Structure of Romantic Nature Imagery," in *The Age of
Johnson: Essays Presented to Chauncey Brewster Tinker* (New Haven, Yale University
Press, 1949), p. 297.
4. Letter to W. Sotheby, Sept. 10, 1802, in *Letters of Samuel Taylor Coleridge*, ed.
Ernest Hartley Coleridge (London, W. Heinemann, 1895), *1*, 404.
5. Good critics have previously recognized that Wordsworth's most significant imagery

consists of symbols. MacNeice, in *Modern Poetry, a Personal Essay,* pp. 91, 113, terms literal images "properties" and remarks that Wordsworth's properties carry their own message. D. G. James, in *The Romantic Comedy* (New York, Oxford University Press, 1948), p. 75, contrasts the ordinary poetic process whereby a poet employs simile or metaphor to give body and precision to his awareness of something not in the sensuous world with Wordsworth's procedure. "Most often, in the poetry of Wordsworth, his perceptions of spiritual realities are reached strictly through excited response to natural scenery. In saying this, I have not in mind that he rejoiced as a 'poet of Nature' in the life and features of the natural world; but that his coming to what he believed to be truth about human life was a process which cannot be separated out from his perception of natural scenery; so that the scene beheld becomes an image of spiritual reality hitherto unknown to him." Ransom, in "William Wordsworth: Notes toward an Understanding of Poetry," in *Wordsworth: Centenary Studies Presented at Cornell and Princeton Universities,* ed. Dunklin, p. 98, calls the literal terms in Wordsworth "spreaders" and comments on their importance in Wordsworth's poetry. Studies previously made of Wordsworth's imagery have, however, not been concerned with this area. Viola Juanita Hill, in "Wordsworth's Imagery and What It Tells Us" (Ph.D. dissertation, University of Indiana, 1947), adopts the method of Caroline Spurgeon in classifying the subject matter which Wordsworth employed in his metaphors and similes. Elisabet Ciesielski in her *Vergleich und Metaphor bei W. Wordsworth* (Marburg, Franz Fischer, 1931) considers only the *Poems of the Imagination* and is concerned primarily with Wordsworth's sense of the transcendental.

III

Landscape—Light and Dark

THAT Wordsworth has two characteristic landscapes is no new discovery, though different writers have chosen to prefer one or the other as that of the real Wordsworth. Matthew Arnold chose to emphasize the joy in Wordsworth,[1] A. C. Bradley pointed to the dark loneliness in him,[2] and much recent criticism has likewise focused on the darkness.[3] Neither side does full justice to Wordsworth's vision of the world, and the confusing point is that Wordsworth's vision in this as in most things was not constant: in the great decade the landscape is predominantly one of light and life and love; before and after appears the darkness. Yet the greatness of the great decade results from Wordsworth's seeing the darkness and the light together, and the troubling aspect of the later poetry is that while "Our haughty life is crowned with darkness," Wordsworth insisted on culling

> Those images of genial beauty, oft
> Too lovely to be pensive in themselves
> But by reflection made so, which do best
> And fitliest serve to crown with fragrant wreaths
> Life's cup when almost filled with years, like mine.[4]

Consequently an attempt to observe Wordsworth's use of the landscape and its changing significance for him amounts in part to tracing the development of Wordsworth's mind. However, since my concern is not with Wordsworth's biography but with landscape as the vehicle of Wordsworth's thought, my structure will be only partially chronological. I propose to examine in turn what I can only call the haunted landscape with its secondary aspects of cold and dreariness, the beloved landscape of light and life and love, and finally the dual landscape. One obvious difficulty of such examination is that landscape overlaps with "Nature," but this difficulty is perhaps evidence of the significance of the study.

1. "Wordsworth," *Essays in Criticism*, Ser. 2 (London, Macmillan, 1888), p. 153.
2. "Wordsworth," *Oxford Lectures in Poetry* (2d ed., London, Macmillan, 1926), pp. 123–4, 141–2.
3. See especially Raymond Dexter Havens, *The Mind of a Poet. A Study of Wordsworth's Thought with Particular Reference to "The Prelude"* (Baltimore, Johns Hopkins Press, 1941), chaps. iii, iv, and James, "Visionary Dreariness," *Scepticism and Poetry*, pp. 141–69.
4. *Musings near Aquapendente*, ll. 200–4.

[Landscape as the vehicle of fear appears in Wordsworth's earliest poetry. Amid its Miltonic echoes and Gothic extravagances *The Vale of Esthwaite*[5] oscillates between landscape objectively described and landscape alive with horrors. Opening with a description the details of which occur again and again in Wordsworth—the mist clearing from the valley but still covering the lake and mountain tops, the shepherd's dog appearing and disappearing into the mist, the cottage "smoking from the trees"—the poem quickly departs from the natural in favor of "brooding Superstition" and "A cold and awful horror." The suffering spirits and grisly phantom are succeeded by a sheep "Starting wildly from its sleep"; the placid twilight passage leads to a night scene of "wild affright" in which a "female form" leads the protagonist to "An iron coffin mark'd with blood." The poem is too immature to warrant a very detailed examination; it is sufficient, I think, to observe the landscape-fear equation that Wordsworth seems to be making. He asserts that "that soul was never blind / To pleasures of a softer kind" but quickly reverts to terror and a "tall thin Spectre" whose "Faint murmuring" may or may not point ahead to the ghastly soldier of *The Prelude.*

In *Guilt and Sorrow, The Borderers,* and *Peter Bell* a somber landscape frames the action and even becomes a part of it. Wordsworth himself referred scornfully to *Guilt and Sorrow,*[6] and the poem is usually dismissed as an inept mixture of sentimental morality and Gothic horror[7] or as a failure consequent on Wordsworth's early lack of narrative skill.[8] Since the poem as we have it represents work not only of 1793–96 but also of 1842,[9] both these comments seem to me to ignore the evolution of the poem. It began as a story of a female vagrant, with the traveler serving no greater function than that of listener. It ended as the sailor's story, with the woman's story subordinated. I should like to advance the theory that whereas in the earliest version the woman's story of her sufferings seems to have little or no connection with the impressive setting that Wordsworth provided for it, the poem, worked over in 1795–96, again in the period when Wordsworth was writing *Peter Bell,* and finally in 1842, became like *Peter Bell* a story of redemption in which the landscape stanzas, instead of being, as Meyer suggests, inartistic lapses, are made to symbolize and objectify the

5. This poem and other *juvenilia* are available only in *PW, 1,* 270 ff.
6. *EL,* pp. 270–2.
7. See Oscar James Campbell and Paul Mueschke, " 'Guilt and Sorrow': A Study in the Genesis of Wordsworth's Aesthetics," *MP, 23* (February, 1926), 293–306.
8. George Wilbur Meyer, *Wordsworth's Formative Years* (Ann Arbor, University of Michigan Press, 1943), p. 146.
9. Four manuscripts of the poem exist, two dating from 1793–96 and two from 1842. The published version of the entire poem appeared in 1842; a version of stanzas XXIII–L was published in 1798 as *The Female Vagrant.* See *PW, 1,* 330–41, and notes to the poem, pp. 94–127.

sailor's inner landscape. The poem does not altogether read as a poem about "the vices of the penal law," whatever Wordsworth's intentions may have been. It reads as a poem about the human soul.

Salisbury Plain stands as the outer symbol of desolation. Across it the traveler for whom there is no room in the inn makes his way, finding no tree, no spot of green, no brook, no sign of human life or habitation. Only the sound of the wind and the flight of crows stir in the vacant waste. But the scene in its desolation is right for the sailor, who has left a murdered man behind him. No place, says Wordsworth, can be too lonely for him. Even here reminder of his crime confronts him, for suddenly he sees a human body swinging on a gibbet.

> It was a spectacle which none might view,
> In spot so savage, but with shuddering pain;
> Nor only did for him at once renew
> All he had feared from man, but roused a train
> Of the mind's phantoms, horrible as vain.
> The stones, as if to cover him from day,
> Rolled at his back along the living plain;
> He fell, and without sense or motion lay;
> But, when the trance was gone, feebly pursued his way.[1]

In these lines, it seems to me, the inner and outer landscapes coalesce; the purpose is not Gothic horror but preparation for a change in the man.[2]

Wandering on in the wind the sailor comes to the desolate structure, the pile of Stonehenge, symbol of the terror and misery nature has long witnessed. No shelter is to be had there and the man goes on, with no moon, no friendly sound, no life or light to be discovered. Finally in all the desolation—the landscape of guilt—he comes upon the "Dead House," a little shelter where "no human being could remain." There in the "naked room" he encounters a fellow sufferer, a woman who can at first view him only with horror. Gothic terror perhaps lingers behind her terror, but how should a man in the state that Wordsworth has been developing be viewed except with fear? Gradually she tells him her own tale of suffering—the loss of her father's land, the time of war and unemployment which followed her marriage, her husband's enlistment, the deaths of husband and children. As she pauses in her tale, weeping, the sailor rises and sees the first streaks of dawn and both are cheered by the "rays of promise." Meyer finds that these stanzas describing the change in weather break into the mood pointlessly;[3] I should like to suggest the possibility that the change in the landscape

1. Stanza x.
2. Cf. Peter Bell's trance, *Peter Bell,* ll. 526–30.
3. *Wordsworth's Formative Years,* p. 147.

indicates the first change in the man's inner landscape of guilt. Compassion for another human is altering the bleak scene. The sailor

> to her pensive cheer
> Tempered fit words of hope; and the lark warbled near.[4]

As the two set out together in the morning sunlight the landscape is still lonely, but

> The barrows glistered bright with drops of rain,
> Whistled the waggoner with merry note,
> The cock far off sounded his clarion throat.[5]

The woman continues her story as they go, telling of her return to England, her hopelessness and starvation, her wandering with thieves, her abuse of herself. Like the sailor she knows guilt, and she sorrows for her knowledge. Despite his own burden the sailor comforts her as best he can, and the two go on. But they encounter a man beating a child and the sailor's humanity again asserts itself as he comforts the child and warns the father:

> "Bad is the world, and hard is the world's law
> Even for the man who wears the warmest fleece;
> Much need have ye that time more closely draw
> The bond of nature, all unkindness cease." [6]

As the sailor voices man's dependence on man, the need for the bond of nature, his own woes are calmed. Finally the wanderers enter a pleasant valley where humanity is kind, and in a rustic cottage the two are fed. But the sailor has one more encounter still with suffering humanity—his own wife is brought in to die. The sailor's bond of nature cannot be denied:

> when, in the hour of death,
> He saw his Wife's lips move his name to bless
> With her last words, unable to suppress
> His anguish, with his heart he ceased to strive;
> And, weeping loud in this extreme distress,
> He cried—"Do pity me! That thou shouldst live
> I neither ask nor wish—forgive me, but forgive!" [7]

His wife dies in peace, the sailor surrenders himself to justice, and the poem ends with a negative recall of the swinging corpse against the stormy sky.

4. Stanza XXXVI, 323–4.
5. Stanza XXXVII, 327–30.
6. Stanza LVII, 505–8.
7. Stanza LXIX, 615–21.

His fate was pitied. Him in iron case
(Reader, forgive the intolerable thought)
They hung not:—no one on *his* form or face
Could gaze, as on a show by idlers sought;
No kindred sufferer, to his death-place brought
By lawless curiosity or chance,
When into storm the evening sky is wrought,
Upon his swinging corse an eye can glance,
And drop, as he once dropped, in miserable trance.

Whether or not Wordsworth meant the sailor's encounters with other suffering humans to act upon the sailor's inner mind,[8] the correspondence of the opening landscape to the inner landscape of guilt seems undeniable. The poem's reliance on sheer coincidence weakens its movement, and the unhappy woman's story—her future left curiously disregarded—seems disproportionately long, as if Wordsworth never completed his shift in focus. What power the poem has—and I think it has a good deal —rises from its powerful portrayal of the desolate landscape of guilt.

The dramatic use of landscape in *The Borderers* to reinforce action has been more generally recognized. Here Marmaduke, the protagonist, is not guilty from the beginning but stands at first between Oswald, the embodiment of the cold unfeeling reason and of monstrous pride, and the Baron Herbert, a blind old man whose sufferings should elicit compassionate aid. The landscape in the opening scenes probably has no great significance, but when the scene shifts to the half-ruined castle —the desolate structure—the use of landscape to reinforce action becomes completely clear. Here the wild storm and the ruined structure of *Guilt and Sorrow* reappear,[9] as Oswald urges on Marmaduke the murder of Herbert. While Herbert sleeps in the castle's dungeon, Marmaduke searches in the abyss of his mind for judgment; his breast "Concentres all the terrors of the Universe." [1] Spared from the actual murder by the objectified forces of conscience—his sense of Oswald's hand on his arm, of Herbert's dead dog Leader tugging at his wrist, of Herbert's resemblance to his daughter Idonea, of the star shining in the sky—Marmaduke later abandons Herbert on a desolate moor that in its barren loneliness sums up man's inhumanity to man. There, where only a tree

That turns its goat's-beard flakes of pea-green moss
From the stern breathing of the rough sea-wind [2]

8. In MS 2 (1795–96) the sailor does not surrender; he is accused by the good cottage pair. But once he has been accused he goes "Not without pleasure" and the stroke that ends his sufferings is "Blest." See De Selincourt's *apparatus criticus, PW, 1,* 126.
9. See also *Fragment of a "Gothic" Tale, PW, 1,* 287 ff.
1. II, 782, 784–5.
2. III, 1295–6.

gives company, he leaves Herbert. The desolate prospect of the scene
in which Herbert sinks exhausted, the deserted chapel on the rocks,
whose bell ringing in the wind has drawn Herbert to it hoping to find
help, seem to symbolize the state of man when natural feelings have been
cut off and only the hard rocks of intellect and pride are left. Properly,
of course, this is Oswald's inner landscape; that it is Herbert who
dies in this wasteland perhaps indicates some confusion in Wordsworth's use of the symbolism. Oswald's story of his own experience,
thereafter told to Marmaduke, when he was led by his crew to abandon
their captain on a bare rock having no grass, no shade, repeats the symbol. The captain was "A man by man cast off," left to die on the naked
rock,[3] just as Herbert was left upon the barren moor. The failure of
human sympathy seems to account for the absence of life in both scenes.

Like *Guilt and Sorrow, The Borderers* is fundamentally grim in its
philosophy. The sailor's crime can be atoned for only by his own death;
Marmaduke's desertion of Herbert leads him to hold himself accursed,
his destiny simply to endure, to wander alone in search of expiation. At
one point in Oswald's story Wordsworth seems almost on the verge of
recognizing that sin can lead to growth, but the idea does not emerge.[4]
Oswald proclaims

> False Shame discarded, spurious Fame despised,
> Twin sisters both of Ignorance, I found
> Life stretched before me smooth as some broad way
> Cleared for a monarch's progress.[5]

But the growth that results in Oswald's case is clearly evil leading to
further evil; evil in Wordsworth's philosophy does not lead to good.
"Strong to o'erturn, strong also to build up" [6] is Oswald's motto, not
Marmaduke's. The possibility of forgiveness never appears.

Wordsworth's nearest approach to the idea of redemption from evil
appears in *Peter Bell* where once again, though less prominently, land-

3. IV, 1727.
4. Much has been written of Wordsworth's debt to Coleridge. It is time, I think, that
someone called attention to the extent to which both *Guilt and Sorrow* and *The Borderers*
anticipate *The Ancient Mariner*. See especially Act IV of *The Borderers*, ll. 1692–1701 of
Oswald's story:
> The wind fell;
> We lay becalmed week after week, until
> The water of the vessel was exhausted;
> I felt a double fever in my veins,
> Yet rage suppressed itself;—to a deep stillness
> Did my pride tame my pride;—for many days,
> On a dead sea under a burning sky,
> I brooded o'er my injuries, deserted
> By man and nature;—if a breeze had blown,
> It might have found its way into my heart.
5. IV, 1834 ff.
6. V, 2277; cf. I, 47.

scape objectifies an inner state of mind. Peter, wild, rude, indifferent
to the primrose by the river's brim, undertakes, as everyone knows, to
steal a solitary ass that he has found in a deserted quarry. But that creature in its contrary fashion refuses to budge, and when Peter, having
beaten its gaunt carcass, threatens to heave the ass into the river, the
ass brays in a fashion that to Peter sounds both joyful and fearful. Driven
by "demoniac power" Peter persists and the ass brays again.

> What is there now in Peter's heart!
> Or whence the might of this strange sound?
> The moon uneasy looked and dimmer,
> The broad blue heavens appeared to glimmer,
> And the rocks staggered all around— [7]

Eventually Peter discovers the corpse of the ass's dead master in the
river, and he, like the sailor of *Guilt and Sorrow,* falls into a trance.
Recovering, he is led on by the ass to draw the body from the river
and to carry the news to the dead man's home. But the ass has only begun to influence Peter. As they journey homeward the lamenting cry
of the dead man's son troubles Peter's already unsettled mind; then

> The rocks that tower on either side
> Build up a wild fantastic scene;
> Temples like those among the Hindoos,
> And mosques, and spires, and abbey-windows,
> And castles all with ivy green!
>
> And while the Ass pursues his way
> Along this solitary dell,
> As pensively his steps advance,
> The mosques and spires change countenance,
> And look at Peter Bell! [8]

In the rest of the poem landscape plays little part. The "Spirits of the
Mind" work on through Peter's sight of blood drops from the ass,
through the ass's disturbing grin at Peter as Peter regains confidence, [9]
and through the coincidence of an underground explosion, all of which
turn him "adrift into the past." Finally, after a hallucinatory vision
of a dead child-wife, Peter hears the voice of a Methodist preacher crying "Repent" and promising forgiveness. Thereupon Peter's animal
self becomes as a little child and the way to his redemption is open.

In *Peter Bell* the landscape is rather like the shining star in *The Borderers;* both represent forces of conscience. Nowhere in *Peter Bell* does

7. Ll. 481–5.
8. Ll. 681–90.
9. The ass seems an agent in Peter's redemption very like Balaam's ass, Numbers **22.**

the landscape seem to objectify an inner world of guilt and of failure in human sympathy as it did in *Guilt and Sorrow* and *The Borderers.* Never again after these early poems is the landscape so desolate and bleak, though the dark world that Wordsworth had seen was never to vanish entirely. Hereafter it is most likely to seem not an objective correlative of an inner state of mind but an independent outer world that exists in its own right. In *The Prelude* landscape possesses an independent life which comes out to meet and act upon the mind.

The scenes from the first book of *The Prelude* in which Wordsworth describes his early awakening to the "sense / Of unknown modes of being" in the universe are so well known that I hesitate to discuss them again.[1] Surely everyone remembers the "Low breathings" and "sounds / Of indistinguishable motion" that pursued the boy Wordsworth after he had stolen a bird from someone else's snare, and the peak "black and huge" that reared its head and towered between the boy in the stolen boat and the stars. From that encounter he carried

> a dim and undetermined sense
> Of unknown modes of being; o'er my thoughts
> There hung a darkness, call it solitude
> Or blank desertion. No familiar shapes
> Remained, no pleasant images of trees,
> Of sea or sky, no colours of green fields;
> But huge and mighty forms, that do not live
> Like living men, moved slowly through the mind
> By day, and were a trouble to my dreams.

To such moments Wordsworth attributes the development of his sense of the "Wisdom and Spirit of the universe!" his sense of the one life that inhabited the mind of man and gave to "forms and images a breath / And everlasting motion."[2] Fear is second to love in stimulating the growth of the mind; religious awareness develops from the ministry of fear.

Equally well known are the dreary landscapes of those famous spots of time from which Wordsworth drew a sense of the creative life in his own mind. The rough and stony moor where a murderer had once been hanged recalls the gibbet image of *Guilt and Sorrow,* though here

> The gibbet-mast had mouldered down, the bones
> And iron case were gone,

and only a name remained carved on the turf. The naked pool lying beneath the hills, the beacon on the summit, the girl beating her way against the wind combined to form a scene of "visionary dreariness."

1. For especially able discussions see references in nn. 2 and 3, p. 28.
2. I, 392–400, 401–4.

Wordsworth recalling the scene knew himself close to the "hiding-places of man's power." [3] Similarly the spot in which the boy watched for the horses that were to come to take him from school for vacation—the single sheep, the one blasted tree, the old stone wall, the mist and wind and sleety rain—in its "Tempestuous, dark, and wild" nature in some way related itself to the workings of his spirit. [4] Both scenes were connected with death, for Wordsworth's father died during the vacation that he had so eagerly awaited. Bradley calls this second scene "apocalyptic" and attributes its power to "the sense of contrast between the narrow world of common pleasures and blind and easy hopes, and the vast unseen world which encloses it in beneficent yet dark and inexorable arms." [5]

There are then in Wordsworth's poetry two quite different landscapes of darkness, the aspects of which are not always altogether distinct. In both *Guilt and Sorrow* and *The Borderers* there is a clearly recognizable wasteland landscape that belongs to or is the consequence of a failure in human sympathy. It is the dark, barren landscape of pride, apartness, and guilt [6]—recognized and rejected in *Lines Left upon a Seat in a Yew-Tree, Which Stands near the Lake of Esthwaite, on a Desolate Part of the Shore, Commanding a Beautiful Prospect*. In this poem the embittered man whom the world had rejected nursed his pride in a desolate spot where his only visitants were "a straggling sheep, / The stone-chat, or the glancing sandpiper" and there found its barren rocks "An emblem of his own unfruitful life." Not content to let the symbolism of the landscape speak for itself, Wordsworth cautions the stranger who reads his lines to remember that "he who feels contempt / For any living thing" is failing to mature, that "true knowledge leads to love." Some of the element of guilt clearly enters into Wordsworth's boyish experience of "unknown modes of being"; the stolen bird and stolen boat are evidence enough. Perhaps it enters too into the strange fascination of the spots of time—the place where the gibbet once was, the place where the boy Wordsworth longed for the vacation in which his

---

3. xii, 237–8, 248–61, 377–80.
4. xii, 292–326, 298, quoted.
5. "Wordsworth," *Oxford Lectures in Poetry*, p. 134.
6. Fausset, Read, and the various other critics who find in Wordsworth's relationship with Annette Vallon the prime source of his guilt seem to me to have read neither their Wordsworth nor their psychology deeply enough. Wordsworth himself, though plainly troubled by the image of a deserted mother, makes very clear that his real trouble lay much deeper, in the alienation from his own feelings that followed the conflict in his mind between his love of England and his hatred of her when she warred against France. When this conflict was followed by a similar love and hatred conflict directed toward France, he turned to abstract philosophy in an effort to do away with feelings altogether. This effort he described as "the crisis of that strong disease," "the soul's last and lowest ebb." *The Prelude*, xi, 306–7. See x, 268–99, 374–415, and xi, 223–305. When Wordsworth recovered spontaneous feeling, he recovered his health.

father's death was unexpectedly to occur. Yet it would be a serious error to see stirring in these moments nothing more than guilt, for here there is clearly present Wordsworth's sense of the dark mystery that surrounds our little world. This second aspect of the dark landscape I can only call religious; whereas the wasteland landscape of guilt may be expected to vanish once Wordsworth's crisis had past, this second kind of darkness would seem to be more permanent.

Yet for a time there was to be little or no darkness in Wordsworth's vision of the world. His landscape was to be drenched with light, overflowing with life, miraculous with love. Although it comes suddenly after the long period of guilt and darkness, this landscape as well as the dark landscape has its beginnings in Wordsworth's earliest poetry. In the *Anacreon* and in *Beauty and Moonlight* landscape images permit the youthful poet to describe his beloved.[7]

The landscape images in the *Anacreon* prove to be, as one would expect, Wordsworth's own.[8] The next to the last verse-paragraph, in which Wordsworth virtually identifies the landscape with the body of his love, is especially interesting, for here there appears the combination of mist and stream, landscape half hidden under mist, and the dream of the happy home amidst it all that was to be a constant image cluster for Wordsworth. The remarkable thing, of course, is the sexual nature of the imagery as Wordsworth uses it here.[9] The absence of sexuality in Wordsworth's poetry has frequently been remarked;[1] in this poem the

7. *PW, 1,* 261–4.

8. See No. 16, "The Anacreontea," in *Elegy and Iambus,* tr. and ed. John Maxwell Edmonds (Loeb Classical Library, London, W. Heinemann, 1931), *2,* 40–2 in the second set of page numbers.

9.   Let thy softest pencil throw
O'er her neck a tint of snow,
There let all the Loves repair,
Let all the Graces flutter there.
Loosely chaste o'er all below
Let the snowy mantle flow,
As silvered by the morning beam
The white mist curls on Grasmere's stream,
Which, like a veil of flowing light,
Hides half the landskip from the sight.
Here I see the wandering rill,
The white flocks sleeping on the hill,
While Fancy paints, beneath the veil,
The pathway winding through the dale,
The cot, the seat of Peace and Love,
Peeping through the tufted grove.

1. See Émile Legouis, *The Early Life of William Wordsworth, 1770–1798,* tr. J. W. Matthews (London, J. M. Dent, 1932), p. 480, where even after the discovery of the Annette affair Legouis maintained that "The Nature he [Wordsworth] celebrates is spiritualized, hence incomplete and in a sense non-existent." See also F. R. Leavis, "Wordsworth," in *Revaluation: Tradition and Development in English Poetry* (London, Chatto & Windus, 1936), pp. 169–71.

landscape itself is identified with a sexual object. In *Beauty and Moonlight* Wordsworth makes similar associations between moonlight on
boughs of yew and swans on the water and the body of his love.[2]

Septimi Gades, which De Selincourt ascribes to 1794,[3] contains the
image of the mist-covered landscape in its more familiar, naturalistic
form. Looking ahead to the time when he and his beloved shall be together, possibly in Grasmere's quiet vale, the poet recalls the charms of
the place, including

> When shouts and sheepfold bells and sounds
> Of flocks and herds and streams rebound
> Along the ringing dale,
> How beauteous, round that gleaming tide,
> The silvery morning vapours glide
> And half the landscape veil.

The young poet thinks

> that morning scene displays
> A lovely emblem of our days,
> Unobvious and serene;
> So shall our still lives, half betrayed,
> Shew charms more touching from their shade,
> Though veiled, yet not unseen.[4]

Further preparation for landscape as the vehicle of love and happiness appears in the fact that landscape in *An Evening Walk* and in *Descriptive Sketches* is the sole compensation for the poet's departed pleasures. Despite the artificiality of Wordsworth's grammar and the endless personification employed in these poems, Wordsworth is already
finding tranquillity and religious awe in the landscape. In *An Evening
Walk* it is "Quiet" that leads the poet up the shady mountain brook, and
the evening scene composes and soothes him.[5] The farewell light of day
blends into night with "religious awe" and the poem ends with the "song
of mountain-streams" heard in the stillness of the evening air.[6] The
emphasis on liberty and freedom in *Descriptive Sketches* should not lead
one to ignore the religious note that is sounded even more clearly than
in *An Evening Walk.* The very fact that whole lines which appear in
the famous description of the Simplon Pass in Book VI of *The Prelude*
originally appeared in *Descriptive Sketches* would seem to point to the

2. For the relation between this poem and Coleridge's *Lewti* see Jane Worthington
Smyser, "Coleridge's Use of Wordsworth's Juvenilia," *PMLA,* 65 (June, 1950), 419–26.
3. *PW, 1,* 371.
4. *Septimi Gades,* stanza 10, 55–60; stanza 11, 61–6.
5. 1793 text, ll. 71, 309–10.
6. Ll. 329, 433 ff.

presence of the germ of the religious intuition in *Descriptive Sketches*.[7]
Such passages as the following sound clearly, it seems to me, the note
that was to come:

> —And sure there is a secret Power that reigns
> Here, where no trace of man the spot profanes,
> Nought but the herds that pasturing upward creep,
> Hung dim-discover'd from the dangerous steep,
> Or summer hamlet, flat and bare, on high
> Suspended, mid the quiet of the sky.
> How still! no irreligious sound or sight
> Rouzes the soul from her severe delight.
> An idle voice the sabbath region fills
> Of Deep that calls to Deep across the hills,
> Broke only by the melancholy sound
> Of drowsy bells for ever tinkling round;
> Faint wail of eagle melting into blue
> Beneath the cliffs, and pine-woods steady sugh;
> The solitary heifer's deepen'd low;
> Or rumbling heard remote of falling snow.[8]

We have already observed the steady lightening of the landscape in
the final sections of *Guilt and Sorrow,* when the sailor recognizes the
"bond of nature," and the use of starlight to objectify the pull of feeling for fellow humanity in *The Borderers.*

Despite such preparations Wordsworth uses landscape as the vehicle
of the divine with such certainty and power in *Tintern Abbey* that one
feels totally unprepared for it by his previous poetry. Familiar as it is,
the imagery of this poem will bear re-examination, for it is the high
point of one aspect of Wordsworth's vision of life. The over-all structure of the poem is built on the time pattern of human life set against
the unchanging landscape. Lines 1–57 recall Wordsworth's former visit
to the scene and what it has meant to him, lines 57–111—except for another brief look backward in lines 65–83—deal with the present, and
lines 111 to the end look to the future. Behind the changing human
being stands the scene, unchanging, permanent, abiding. What Wordsworth does with the scene, of course, makes the poem, for while the poem
begins and ends with the natural scene—"These steep woods and lofty
cliffs, / And this green pastoral landscape"—the central section has
made of the landscape a symbol of that which abides.

From the very beginning Wordsworth subtly idealizes the outer,

---

7. Cf. *The Prelude,* VI, 561, and *Descriptive Sketches,* l. 130; *The Prelude,* VI, 563-4,
and *Descriptive Sketches,* ll. 249-50.
8. 1793 text, ll. 424-39; see also ll. 542-9.

visible landscape to evoke a world alive with spirit in which man and nature alike are part of the same life. The steep, lofty cliffs along the bank of the Wye

> on a wild secluded scene impress
> Thoughts of more deep seclusion; and connect
> The landscape with the quiet of the sky.

Thus Wordsworth directly links the visible scene with thoughts and at the same time suggests by "the quiet of the sky" the spiritual meaning that the landscape holds for him. As he looks out over the scene before him human and natural merge together, for the orchard tufts with their unripe fruits

> Are clad in one green hue, and lose themselves
> 'Mid groves and copses.[9]

The very hedgerows seem like so much "sportive wood run wild"; the farms "Green to the very door" can hardly be distinguished. The silent smoke wreaths among the trees seem to come not from habitations but from vagrants in the woods or from some hermit's cave. In other words, the thoughts of more deep seclusion have prevailed. Even in what seems literal description of the scene before him Wordsworth has so merged farms and woods together in one green hue and so emphasized the silence and seclusion of the scene that one is prepared to deal with more than literal landscape.

Thus the shift to Wordsworth's own mind, to the value these "beauteous forms" have previously held for him, is not abrupt. The sweet sensations, the feelings of pleasure, and the blessed mood in which one sees into the life of things rise in sequence from the purely organic to the merging once again of human and natural. The sensations felt in the blood and along the heart and even in the purer mind bring restoration; the feelings of unremembered pleasure have led to unremembered acts of kindness. The final gift, the blessed mood

> In which the burthen of the mystery,
> In which the heavy and the weary weight
> Of all this unintelligible world,
> Is lightened:—that serene and blessed mood,
> In which the affections gently lead us on,—
> Until, the breath of this corporeal frame
> And even the motion of our human blood
> Almost suspended, we are laid asleep
> In body, and become a living soul:[1]

9. Ll. 13–14.
1. Ll. 38–46.

leads once more to the natural world—we see into the life of things. Just
as the blending of orchards and woods in one green hue has previously
eliminated all conflict, so here the eye is made quiet and raised to
spiritual insight. Previously the human seemed submerged in the natural; here the human is once again submerged, but with the difference that in the mood of mystic insight the world of things becomes
alive.

Turning to the present, Wordsworth recognizes that he is no longer
the tempestuous youth who once bounded over the mountains passion-
ately absorbed in sounding cataract and rock and wood. Once again
the verse rises effortlessly from the literal scene to its deeper significance;
this time the literal is minimized and the deeper significance binds human and natural in a spiritual union. Nature from having been a feeling and a love sufficient has come to hold

> The still, sad music of humanity,
> Nor harsh nor grating, though of ample power
> To chasten and subdue.

And he has felt

> A presence that disturbs me with the joy
> Of elevated thoughts; a sense sublime
> Of something far more deeply interfused,
> Whose dwelling is the light of setting suns,
> And the round ocean and the living air,
> And the blue sky, and in the mind of man:
> A motion and a spirit, that impels
> All thinking things, all objects of all thought,
> And rolls through all things.[2]

Therefore he loves the woods and mountains, the mighty world the
senses half create and half perceive; therefore he recognizes in nature
the soul of all his moral being.

It is worth reiterating, I think, that one accepts this statement of the
spiritual union of man and nature because of the way in which Wordsworth has in the preceding sections of the poem connected the landscape with the quiet of the sky and merged human into natural. Eye and
ear truly half create: the eye perceives the hedgerows and creates the
picture of sportive little lines of wood running wild; the eye perceives
the smoke wreaths and creates the vagrants in the houseless woods. The
natural is endowed with life even before the spiritual eye sees into the
life of things: the plots of ground and orchards are *clad* in one green
hue; the hedgerows are *sportive* and *run;* the Wye is a *wanderer.*

The last section of the poem looks ahead to the future and gradually

2. Ll. 91–3, 94–102.

lowers the tone until one returns to the literal steep wood and lofty cliffs from which the poem began. Nature can strengthen man,

> for she can so inform
> The mind that is within us, so impress
> With quietness and beauty, and so feed
> With lofty thoughts, that neither evil tongues,
> Rash judgments, nor the sneers of selfish men,
> Nor greetings where no kindness is, nor all
> The dreary intercourse of daily life,
> Shall e'er prevail against us.[3]

Said of literal rocks and trees this would seem to be nonsense. Said in connection with Nature as the dwelling place of the divine the metaphors carry conviction. The heavy and the weary weight of this unkind world cannot prevail against the mind informed by the divine presence. Therefore Wordsworth exhorts his sister to walk alone in the moonlight and take pleasure in the mountain winds so that if ever trouble befalls her she will have stored in her mind lovely forms and sweet sounds and harmonies for healing. Weaver's objection that in the conclusion of the poem Wordsworth "comes down dizzily into sensism" [4] ignores the structural curve of the poem, its rise from the quiet matter-of-fact to the sublime and its return to the quiet and natural.[5]

Wordsworth's imagery in *Tintern Abbey* tends to idealize, to harmonize, to unify. His subject is the past, present, and future significance of the scene that he beholds; as he dwells on the wild green landscape, human and natural blend into one idealized whole in which the one life lives and moves and has its being. The sense of the one life pulses through the *Lyrical Ballads* of 1798 and 1800 and into the *Poems* of 1807, irradiating their landscape. The rebirth that Wordsworth had experienced after his long unhappy introversion bore its fruit in the overwhelming intuition of light and life and love. *To My Sister, Lines Written in Early Spring, Expostulation and Reply,* and *The Tables Turned* state and restate Wordsworth's awareness of the one life and his belief in the value of intuition as the best way of experiencing that life.

> Love, now an universal birth,
> From heart to heart is stealing,

3. Ll. 125–32.
4. Bennett Weaver, "Wordsworth: The Growth of a Poet's Mind," *Papers of the Michigan Academy of Science, Arts, and Letters, 24* (1938), 116.
5. Cf. the interpretation of *Tintern Abbey* given by James Benziger in *"Tintern Abbey* Revisited," *PMLA, 65* (March, 1950), 154–62. Benziger finds the same interfusion of human, natural, and divine that I do; he emphasizes, however, not spiritual life but the Divine Quiet and finds the poem "quietistic." See also Henry J. W. Milley, "Some Notes on Coleridge's 'Eolian Harp,'" *MP, 36* (May, 1939), 368–9, who points out that Coleridge in *The Eolian Harp* originated the form which Wordsworth uses in *Tintern Abbey.*

From earth to man, from man to earth:
—It is the hour of feeling.

Through primrose tufts, in that green bower,
The periwinkle trailed its wreaths;
And 'tis my faith that every flower
Enjoys the air it breathes.

The eye—it cannot choose but see;
We cannot bid the ear be still;
Our bodies feel, where'er they be,
Against or with our will.

Nor less I deem that there are Powers
Which of themselves our minds impress;
That we can feed this mind of ours
In a wise passiveness.

And that so often misread defense of intuition and protest against the "meddling intellect": [6]

One impulse from a vernal wood
May teach you more of man,
Of moral evil and of good,
Than all the sages can.

Sweet is the lore which Nature brings;
Our meddling intellect
Mis-shapes the beauteous forms of things:—
We murder to dissect.

Landscape imagery of the purely happy sort decreases in importance after the *Lyrical Ballads* of 1798. It is present in the volume of 1800 largely in the *Poems on the Naming of Places:* except for these, the new poems of 1800 are close to being poems about persons. In the *Poems on the Naming of Places* places and persons are being identified; landscape is losing some of its own unique life. "It was an April morning" repeats most strongly the sense of landscape alive and active as a presence:

The spirit of enjoyment and desire,
And hopes and wishes, from all living things
Went circling, like a multitude of sounds.[7]

6. For an admirable summary of the controversy about these poems see James Venable Logan, *Wordsworthian Criticism: A Guide and Bibliography* (Columbus, Ohio State University, 1947), p. 109, n. 5.
7. Ll. 6–8.

There was "Such an entire contentment in the air" that even the leaf-less trees did not look barren. As the poet happily wandered up the brook he seemed to hear all Nature singing a joyous song: the sound of the brook mingled with the sounds of birds and even the dog's bark-ing, and it all seemed like

> the wild growth
> Or like some natural produce of the air,
> That could not cease to be.

The very rocks seemed to be bursting into leaves, and the song of life found its center in the single mountain cottage that Wordsworth dedi-cated to his sister. In *To Joanna* the poet tells how he was ravished by a scene of flowering broom growing from base to summit of a tall rock; the sight held him motionless, looking. The lady laughed at his delight and the poet half laughingly recalls how the mountains sounded and resounded her laughter. There was, he insists, a "loud uproar in the hills." Dorothy has given William's name to the lonely hilltop that is in truth "The loneliest place we have among the clouds." William has named for Mary the still pool among the beeches that in its deep peace seems made by Nature for herself.

Wordsworth's tendency to identify landscape with a person is per-haps nowhere stronger than in the celebrated Lucy poems. Despite the numerous attempts of critics to identify Lucy with a real person,[8] Lucy seems the living embodiment of English landscape. She is the flower that grows on English ground, guarded by the "overseeing power" that kindles or restrains.

Outside of these poems landscape lingers in the 1800 volume as an in-definable presence. In *Hart-Leap Well* the ruins of Sir Walter's pleasure house, built in his unfeeling pride of conquest over the dead hart, make a doleful scene

> as if the spring-time came not here,
> And Nature here were willing to decay.

The "Powers / Which of themselves our minds impress" live in this spot:

8. Lucy has been variously identified as Mary Hutchinson, Dorothy, Lucy Gray, Hartley Coleridge, etc. Both Arthur Beatty, in *Wordsworth: Representative Poems*, ed. Arthur Beatty (Garden City, Doubleday, Doran, 1937), p. 318, and Herbert Hartman, in "Wordsworth's 'Lucy Poems,'" *PMLA*, 49 (1934), 134–42, remind us that the name "Lucy" was a commonplace in eighteenth-century elegiac poems. Beatty contends, how-ever, that "I travelled among unknown men" was addressed to Mary Hutchinson and that therefore the whole series was probably addressed to her. I do not agree. The fact that the name "Lucy" occurs in the original version of *Nutting*, *PW, 2*, 505, and that *The Prelude* lines, xi, A, 199–221 (see pp. 592–3, nn.) part of which De Selincourt says are an overflow from *Nutting* clearly refer to Dorothy perhaps indicates that if Lucy had a human counterpart it was in Dorothy. The Lucy of "Among all lovely things my Love had been" is also Dorothy.

The Being that is in the clouds and air,
That is in the green leaves among the groves,
Maintains a deep and reverential care
For the unoffending creatures whom he loves.[9]

The poet's ravishment by the scene of *To Joanna* has its reversal in
Nutting, in which the poet recalls a day from his boyhood—"One of
those heavenly days that cannot die"—when he made his way to the
virgin scene of hazelnuts

And dragged to earth both branch and bough, with crash
And merciless ravage: and the shady nook
Of hazels, and the green and mossy bower,
Deformed and sullied, patiently gave up
Their quiet being.[1]

The "spirit in the woods" seems akin to the

spirit and pulse of good,
A life and soul, to every mode of being
Inseparably linked [2]

which embraces in its goodness even the old Cumberland beggar.
    The volume of 1807 includes poems that have the sense of the radiant
joyousness of the outer world and also poems that mark the loss of that
sense. The lines *Written in March* seem a pure distillation of the sense
of joyous life abounding.

The Cock is crowing,
The stream is flowing,
The small birds twitter,
The lake doth glitter,
The green field sleeps in the sun;
The oldest and youngest
Are at work with the strongest;
The cattle are grazing,
Their heads never raising;
There are forty feeding like one!

Flowers, birds, butterflies, all growing and living things sound the note
of love and joy. The small celandine is a "Prophet of delight and mirth"
whose "glittering countenance" is like the spreading rays of the sun.[3]
The little daisy sheds "A happy, genial influence, / Coming one knows
not how, nor whence"; the poet plays with similes and returns to the

9. II, 19–20, 69–72.
1. Ll. 44–8.
2. *The Old Cumberland Beggar,* ll. 77–9.
3. *To the Small Celandine,* l. 57, and *To the Same Flower,* ll. 13–16.

sufficient name *"Flower,"* finding in the daisy's humble brightness a function "apostolical." [4] The green linnet is "A Life, a Presence like the Air," scattering its gladness. The well-known daffodils dance by the waves in glee; the kitten sports with the withered leaves. [5] Some at least of the joyous gleam of this volume comes, however, reflected from earlier years: the chance-discovered sight of bright blue sparrow's eggs "Gleamed like a vision of delight" largely because of the associations they had for Wordsworth with his childhood and with Dorothy. [6] Similarly the two poems addressed *To a Butterfly* reflect partly present joy but more importantly the sunshine and song of "summer days, when we were young."

Helen Darbishire comments that this volume shows Wordsworth's returning again into himself after the "effort of projection" of the *Lyrical Ballads*. [7] Certainly there seems to be in this volume a note of effort, as if the full sun of love which had so irradiated the landscape were diminishing in warmth and light. The poet watching the kitten and his laughing baby resolves that he will have his

> careless season
> Spite of melancholy reason,
> Will walk through life in such a way
> That, when time brings on decay,
> Now and then I may possess
> Hours of perfect gladsomeness. [8]

The *Ode to Duty* admits that Wordsworth can no longer "in love and truth" rely simply on "the genial sense of youth"; the time has not yet come, he says, when love will be an unerring light "And joy its own security." Thus he turns to duty, proclaiming that even the flowers and stars move under its rule. The poem *To a Sky-Lark* (Up with me!) admits that the poet has "walked through wildernesses dreary" and, while the poet resolves to share the lark's joy, he nevertheless pictures himself as plodding on. *Resolution and Independence* describes as perfect a day as one could hope to have, with the sun shining after the night's rain and the birds singing in distant woods.

> All things that love the sun are out of doors;
> The sky rejoices in the morning's birth;
> The grass is bright with rain-drops;—on the moors

---

4. *To the Daisy*, ll. 70–1; *To the Same Flower;* and *To the Daisy* (Bright Flower), l. 23.

5. *The Green Linnet*, l. 21; "I wandered lonely as a cloud"; *The Kitten and Falling Leaves.*

6. *The Sparrow's Nest*, l. 4.

7. "Introduction," *Wordsworth's Poems in Two Volumes, 1807*, ed. Helen Darbishire, p. xl.

8. *The Kitten and Falling Leaves*, ll. 111–16.

The hare is running races in her mirth;
And with her feet she from the plashy earth
Raises a mist; that, glittering in the sun,
Runs with her all the way, wherever she doth run.

But the poet himself falls from joy to melancholy, "Dim sadness—and blind thoughts." [9] The figure who appears to end this mood is no part of my present subject; it is relevant, however, that once the poet's mood has changed the joyous landscape has become "that naked wilderness." [1] The world is too much with us and Wordsworth himself is forlorn, feeling unresponsive to winds and sea. *A Complaint* is perhaps part of the reason, for Coleridge's love, once a fountain at the heart's door, has ceased to flow. Wordsworth seems to be deliberately withdrawing, preferring silence to personal talk and keeping his little boat rocking peaceably by retreating to the world of dreams and books.[2] *Elegiac Stanzas Suggested by a Picture of Peele Castle* gives more of the reason. Never again will Wordsworth see the world irradiated as it once seemed to him. The "tranquil land," the "sky of bliss" have in the shock of his brother's death vanished so that he praises Beaumont's painting of the angry sea and the dismal shore. Strangely enough, Wordsworth equates his former vision of "silent Nature's breathing life" with the kind of happiness that has existed detached from human life; he envies the huge castle of the painting its "unfeeling armour of old time" and resolves to "welcome fortitude, and patient cheer." [3]

The real end of the landscape of light comes, of course, with the *Intimations* ode. As Cleanth Brooks has so admirably noted, there the celestial light, the glory and the dream, fade not to darkness but to the light of common day [4] as the prison of the self closes in upon the growing child. When our life's star under its earthly freight becomes dimmed so that it no longer irradiates every common sight with its glory, Wordsworth is obliged to renounce the mighty world of eye and ear. Questioning sense and outward things, he turns to worlds not realized; our birth is "a sleep and a forgetting" and the grave is a "living place." [5] Eternity has ceased, so far as the landscape goes, to be present here and now.

I am tempted to assert flatly that from this point on landscape ceases to be a significant vehicle in Wordsworth's poetry. Certainly landscape

9. Stanza II; l. 28.
1. *PW*, 2, 237, n., MS reading.
2. *Personal Talk*, I and IV.
3. Why Wordsworth confused his landscape of love with a life of selfishness I do not know, but I am certain that it is a confusion. All his life Wordsworth was to reproach himself from time to time for his detachment—love, as he well knew, was the only solution to human isolation. See *Highland Hut, On the Frith of Clyde,* and "Though the bold wings of Poesy affect."
4. "Wordsworth and the Paradox of the Imagination," *The Well Wrought Urn,* pp. 117–20.
5. *PW, 4, apparatus criticus,* MS M.

as the living, breathing body of the divine ceases to appear; in its place come landscape structures, architectural images that Knight refers to as eternity structures.[6] Certainly landscape imagery in *The Excursion* is disappointing in its failure to realize the promise implicit in Book I.[7] The opening scene in which the Poet toils with languid steps baffled by the slippery turf across a bare wide common under the hot summer sun conveys a sense of fatigue and effort that has no significance as the poem develops. The narrative has—ostensibly—nothing to do with the speaker's own state of mind.

Viewed as an excursion, the journey seems to go as nearly as possible out of this world. The Poet and the Wanderer know from the beginning of the journey that

> what we feel of sorrow and despair
> From ruin and from change, and all the grief
> That passing shows of Being leave behind

is little more than an idle dream. Margaret sleeps in the calm earth and her ruined cottage is peaceful. Our life is but "a sleep and a forgetting," and reality is not in the things of this world. Passing by the festive May-day throng, Poet and Wanderer set out to visit the Solitary, a soul "Lonesome and lost," [8] embittered by the loss of wife and children and subsequent disillusionment in the outcome of the French Revolution.

Climbing amid a savage region they come to "a little lowly vale" enclosed by the mountains, "shut out from all the world!" Enclosed by rocks, trees, "with two green fields, / A liquid pool . . . / And one bare dwelling," the scene impresses the poet as a sweet recess, lonesome and perfectly secure. Just as he thinks to himself that peace exists there or nowhere, ironically there rises from the valley the solemn sound of a funeral dirge. This turns out to have been not for the Solitary, as they fear, for shortly they encounter him attempting to comfort a grieving child. The Solitary is "all fire" at sight of his visitors and explains that the dirge was for a poor old man who has really died because of the thoughtlessness of the housewife in whose dwelling the Solitary resides. As he describes how he searched for the old man he relates a cloud vision that he saw on the return home. Once again, as in *Guilt and Sorrow,* Wordsworth seems to be connecting an act of kindness to a fellow creature with brightening of the landscape, only here it is not so much that the landscape of this world is brightened as that the Solitary has a momentary vision of the next world. A mighty city rose before him in the sky—

6. G. Wilson Knight, "The Wordsworthian Profundity," in *The Starlit Dome* (New York, Oxford University Press, 1941), pp. 61 ff.

7. For a discussion of Book I see below, pp. 60–1.

8. I, 949–53; II, 160.

> marvellous array
> Of temple, palace, citadel, and huge
> Fantastic pomp of structure without name.

As he beheld "the revealed abode / Of Spirits in beatitude" the Solitary too for a moment recognized that the life of this world is not life but death.[9] Since in this one vision Wordsworth has conveyed all splendor imaginable, it is not surprising that there is no repetition or development of the vision. Furthermore, because the vision is unrelated to the Solitary's psychic landscape, it seems a set piece rather than an integral part of the story.

The persistence with which the imagery of *The Excursion* points away from this world has perhaps never been sufficiently observed. The landscape of *Tintern Abbey* speaks of the abiding presence that rolls through all things; the landscape of *The Excursion* gives "shadowy intimations"

> Of purposes akin to those of Man,
> But wrought with mightier arm than now prevails.

Poet, Wanderer, and Solitary together explore the valley and come upon a waterfall over the surface of a crag. The Wanderer hails it:

> —Voiceless the stream descends into the gulf
> With timid lapse;—and lo! while in this strait
> I stand—the chasm of sky above my head
> Is heaven's profoundest azure; no domain
> For fickle, short-lived clouds to occupy,
> Or to pass through; but rather an abyss
> In which the everlasting stars abide.

Eternity presses in upon time and nature, and mortal flux vanishes in its silence. The Solitary, who cannot see beyond his sense "Of instability, revolt, decay, / And change," finds rather that the scene and its freaks of nature feed "Pity and scorn, and melancholy pride," yet he too yearns for peace, "The central feeling of all happiness." The spot where they talk is a "place / Of stillness and close privacy" that seems made for confession, and the Solitary's confession ends in the hope that his "particular current soon will reach / The unfathomable gulf, where all is still." [1]

As the Wanderer answers the Solitary's complaint, the center of gravity of the poem moves even more clearly outside this world. The mind of man is no longer the main region of Wordsworth's song; there is no balance of inner and outer worlds but a complete dependence of inner upon an outer existing outside time and space. The outer world

9. II, 328–49, 516, 832–77.
1. III, 90–8, 138–42, 382, 470–1, 990–1.

of eye and ear is rejected just as the mind of man is rejected; the dependence is upon the supreme will of God. The Wanderer praises the visible world as a temple in which he worships, preserving his "particle divine" and seeking "Repose and hope among eternal things." [2] Wordsworth, who had once known what it was for a mind to be exalted

> by an underpresence,
> The sense of God, or whatsoe'er is dim
> Or vast in its own being [3]

and had possessed a powerful sense of divine immanence, here has the Wanderer direct the Solitary to

> the measures and the forms,
> Which an abstract intelligence supplies;
> Whose kingdom is, where time and space are not.[4]

The landscape of *The Excursion* consequently is a landscape from which life increasingly departs; after Book I the scenic descriptions seem static backdrops for conversation, set pieces inserted at intervals, lacking organic connection. The three companions talking together pace a plot of green that is like the deck of a ship. Stillness surrounds them as the sea surrounds the ship; they voyage toward "regions yet more tranquil." The voice of the lamb bleating as they talk resembles "The plaintive spirit of the solitude"; it seems like the Wanderer's voice crying into the eternal silence. Like the sound of a murmuring stream that flows into the sea, the voice of the Wanderer murmurs of the "abyss / Of infinite Being." Man's soul, says the Wanderer, has the power to transmute error and disappointment and guilt into virtue even as the moonlight turns the dark leaves on which it sheds its light. The whole universe sings of eternity as a shell sings of the sea; when evening makes of the visible world a closed temple the whispering air and the solitary raven alike speak of the eternal.[5]

Once the Wanderer's long argument ceases, the three companions leave the deep valley that is "Like the fixed centre of a troubled world." The scene shifts to a village churchyard where the Solitary asks that the prospect of the soul be placed

> In sober contrast with reality,
> And man's substantial life.

Poet, Wanderer, and Solitary are now joined by the Pastor, who takes the images of reality that follow from the dead lying in the churchyard.

2. IV, 51, 63.
3. *The Prelude*, XIII, A, 71–3.
4. *The Excursion*, IV, 74–6.
5. IV, 253, 412, 891–3, 993–4, 1062 ff., 1132 ff., 1156 ff.

For their previous abstractions the Pastor is to give them solid facts
to help them learn

> *To prize the breath we share with human kind;*
> *And look upon the dust of man with awe.*[6]

While the Pastor relates successive stories of human lives, the landscape is steadily that of the churchyard among the mountains. The
eternity symbols loom on the horizon and lie at the speaker's feet; human
life in the light of eternity loses much of its sting. The Pastor's voice
sounds on like a stream, leaving upon the shore of memory "images and
precious thoughts" of "The native grandeur of the human soul." [7]

It should be observed that although the landscape images of *The
Excursion* seem like set pieces, landscape is still being used symbolically,
with the difference that the tenor symbolized has become transcendent
instead of immanent divinity. The difficulty perhaps is that landscape is
an arbitrary and unnatural symbol of transcendent divinity. Landscape
in *Guilt and Sorrow* successfully objectifies the psychic world; landscape in *Tintern Abbey* successfully provides a natural symbol for immanent divinity; landscape in *The Prelude* combines both these functions; but landscape seems ill adapted to convey

> the measures and the forms,
>
>   .   .   .
>
> Whose kingdom is, where time and space are not.

There is little to be said, consequently, about the landscape of light
in Wordsworth's later poetry except to reaffirm what everyone knows
—its absence. Interest in landscape has become flatly naturalistic; the
landscape is not a vehicle in such poems as *Yarrow Visited,* though the
sunshine of fancy plays on the actual scene. Reality suffers by contrast with the image of the mind; the genuine image will heighten
joy and relieve sorrow but it does so simply as a literal image. *Yarrow
Revisited* sets, like *Tintern Abbey,* the immutable landscape against
the mutability of man, but what Wordsworth praises is the Muse.

> Yea, what were mighty Nature's self?
> Her features, could they win us,
> Unhelped by the poetic voice
> That hourly speaks within us? [8]

The disturbing aspect of this period is the extent to which Wordsworth
denies his former insight:

6. v, 16, 248–9, 656–7.
7. VII, 29; VI, 666.
8, Ll. 85–8.

—There is a radiant though a short-lived flame,
That burns for Poets in the dawning east;
And oft my soul hath kindled at the same,
When the captivity of sleep had ceased;
But He who fixed immoveably the frame
Of the round world, and built, by laws as strong,
   A solid refuge for distress—
   The towers of righteousness;
He knows that from a holier altar came
The quickening spark of this day's sacrifice.[9]

Though along with the "towers of righteousness" Wordsworth recognizes "the abyss of weakness," this ode ends with meditations

Of mysteries revealed,
And judgments unrepealed,
Of earthly revolution,
And final retribution.[1]

From *Laodamia* to the *Sonnets upon the Punishment of Death* the shadow of retribution darkens Wordsworth's later poetry.

The lines *Composed upon an Evening of Extraordinary Splendour and Beauty* in which Wordsworth once again beholds the visionary splendor make clear the change in his vision. In the evening light the distant scene on the mountainside seems near at hand; the antlers of the animals glisten and "gilded flocks appear." Yet Wordsworth cannot believe that the magnificence is solely that of the evening light.

—From worlds not quickened by the sun
A portion of the gift is won.[2]

The mountain ridges aglow in the light seem to show the steps to heaven. Wordsworth remembers "the light / Full early lost, and fruitlessly deplored" but he does not expect to rediscover its source. The source has been externalized and belongs to heavenly regions.

Nor does one find in the later poetry much sense of the dark mystery that encompasses our life. What appears is more akin to the wasteland than to the mysterious religious darkness. In both the second *Ode to Lycoris* (Enough of climbing toil!) and *The Pass of Kirkstone* the world appears shriveled; Wordsworth speaks of "Unacceptable feelings of contempt," but withdraws into "the domains of tender memory." [3] The personified Hope, Joy, and Faith of the final stanza of *The Pass*

9. *Thanksgiving Ode*, ll. 43–52.
1. *Thanksgiving Ode*, ll. 86, 238–41.
2. Ll. 37–8.
3. "Enough of climbing toil!" ll. 8, 51.

of Kirkstone do not carry conviction, so strong has been the picture of the barrenness of life. Nothing is of value—

> Lawns, houses, chattels, groves, and fields,
> All that the fertile valley shields;
> Wages of folly—baits of crime,
> Of life's uneasy game the stake,
> Playthings that keep the eyes awake
> Of drowsy, dotard Time.[4]

The sense of grim endurance is strongest in the poem *To Enterprise.* The "fixed resolves by Reason justified" cleave to their object like sleet

> Whitening a pine tree's northern side,
> When fields are naked far and wide,
> And withered leaves, from earth's cold breast
> Up-caught in whirlwinds, nowhere can find rest.[5]

Even in *Vernal Ode* the stars suggest a vision of endurance, here combined with repose;[6] the springtime life is inseparable from thoughts of transience and mortality.

Wordsworth's most permanently satisfying poetry, it seems to me, does not belong to either the dark or bright patterns but holds together in one vision both dark and bright. Solitude, darkness, and the barren, stony wasteland in some poems fuse with life and light and joy; these are the poems in which dreariness is visionary and life is seen whole. Few poems, of course, combine all the components of both patterns, but wherever solitude and joy, or darkness and light, or the wasteland and life somehow merge, the vision has complexity and depth.

Tintern Abbey, as we have seen, primarily presents the landscape as the abiding symbol of the one life and so belongs to the pattern of life and love. But the poem has a secondary theme set against the dominant one of rapturous devotion. The five winters have been long, the sycamore is dark, the poet has been in lonely rooms amid the din of towns. The unintelligible world is a heavy and a weary weight, a place in which daylight has often been joyless, and in which the fretful stir is unprofitable. *Tintern Abbey* is the impressive poem that it is because it sounds its song of faith and confidence without ignoring the still sad music of humanity.

Likewise *The Prelude* speaks of beauty and of fear, sometimes separately but most impressively when simultaneously.

> The mind of Man is fram'd even like the breath
> And harmony of music. There is a dark

4. Ll. 27–32.
5. Ll. 127–32.
6. L. 47.

Invisible workmanship that reconciles
Discordant elements, and makes them move
In one society.

Pain and fear were sanctified as they evoked the "Presences of Nature,"
the "Souls of lonely places." Projected terror could make the universe
alive: when the solitary boy in the stolen boat rowed in the moonlight,
the huge black peak that towered up seemed a living thing; afterward
the mighty forms that troubled the boy's dreams were unknown modes
of being. Such acute fear was not necessary to evoke the sense of a
living world. November days, when blowing mist "made / A lonely
scene more lonesome," and the solitude of woods and gloomy hills likewise helped the boy to discover the breath and everlasting motion of
forms and images. Skating through cold and darkness while the orange
sky of evening died away, Wordsworth sometimes stopped short upon
his heels to watch the solitary cliffs wheel by, as if the earth's diurnal
round were visible.[7] In all these experiences solitude and light and
darkness and life merged in an experience of "otherness" that extended
the horizons of his mind.[8] Fundamentally these moments are religious,
though Wordsworth does not always make the emotion explicit. In the
moldering abbey of St. Mary an invisible bird sang in the gloom; on
the return from a visit to a tavern the band of boys left one of their
number to blow his flute alone upon the rock. Wordsworth says only
that thus were his sympathies enlarged. "The ghostly language of the
ancient earth" spoke at night in the winds; the song of life rose most
clearly, however, when the fleshly ear,

O'ercome by humblest prelude of that strain,
Forgot her functions, and slept undisturbed.[9]

Perhaps because of the lack of solitude such moments were rare once
the poet entered Cambridge, though even there he tended to live in
his own world, responsive to the terror, love, and beauty of "Nature's
daily face." [1] During his return to Hawkshead in the summer vacation,
however, occurred another of the solitary moments in which Wordsworth experienced the Presence. Walking around the little lake one
cold raw evening, he found himself strengthened and restored with
swellings of the spirit, "glimmering views / How life pervades the un-
decaying mind." So musing, he rested in a wood while darkness slowly
descended, and the hazel leaves about him, moved by the wind, seemed
to be breathing audibly.[2]

7. I, A, 351–5; I, 464, 466, 357 ff., 401–22, 425–63.
8. See Charles Williams, "Wordsworth," *The English Poetic Mind* (Oxford, Clarendon Press, 1932), p. 159.
9. II, 115 ff., 164 ff., 175, 306 ff., 417–19.
1. III, 136 ff.
2. IV, 137–90.

There seems no need to summarize further the extent to which *The Prelude* records this double vision. Probably the most impressive instance of it is the well-known description of the descent from the Alps, when the road followed a narrow chasm:

> The brook and road
> Were fellow-travellers in this gloomy strait,
> And with them did we journey several hours
> At a slow pace. The immeasurable height
> Of woods decaying, never to be decayed,
> The stationary blasts of waterfalls,
> And in the narrow rent at every turn
> Winds thwarting winds, bewildered and forlorn,
> The torrents shooting from the clear blue sky,
> The rocks that muttered close upon our ears,
> Black drizzling crags that spake by the way-side
> As if a voice were in them, the sick sight
> And giddy prospect of the raving stream,
> The unfettered clouds and region of the Heavens,
> Tumult and peace, the darkness and the light—
> Were all like workings of one mind, the features
> Of the same face, blossoms upon one tree;
> Characters of the great Apocalypse,
> The types and symbols of Eternity,
> Of first, and last, and midst, and without end.[3]

Here the changing remains unchanged, the moving does not depart, light shines above and into darkness. The vision from Mount Snowdon of moonlight on the sea of mist that lay above the dusky hills and above the Atlantic, with the silence broken by the roar of waters rising through a rift in the mist, likewise combines a sense of infinity with the sense of dark abysmal depths. To Wordsworth it seemed the image of the mind itself, brooding over its own depths, listening for its own voices, and the shaping moonlight the express resemblance of the shaping spirit of imagination.[4]

The Lucy poems, *Michael, The Brothers, Resolution and Independence, Glen Almain, Stepping Westward, The Solitary Reaper,* and *The Highland Girl*—the poems that exemplify Wordsworth's dual vision— are the best loved and the best known. In all these come elements of darkness—Lucy's death, Michael's solitude, James' death, the dim sadness and blind thoughts of *Resolution and Independence,* the loneliness of the narrow glen, the solitude of the reaper and of the Highland girl.

3 VI, 621–40.
4. XIV, 39–90. In the A text (XIII, 71–3) the infinite is definitely within the mind itself; in the 1850 version the location of the dark abyss is uncertain but the power to be gained is "transcendent" (l. 75).

But in all these poems the dark elements are as it were held in solution: light and life and love contain the darkness and solitude and death. Lucy has died but her death is a return to the great life of nature;

> No motion has she now, no force;
>   She neither hears nor sees;
> Rolled round in earth's diurnal course,
>   With rocks, and stones, and trees.

The poet equates motion with life: the motionless girl has become part of the living motion of the earth, and the poignancy of the poem rises from the poet's awareness of death-within-life.[5]

Michael is perhaps the finest example of this balance. The hidden valley in which Michael lived is now an utter solitude; he who journeys there finds only a few sheep, "with rocks and stones, and kites / That overhead are sailing in the sky." [6] Beside the brook lies a stone pile, "a straggling heap of unhewn stones!" This stone pile is the central image of the poem; with it Wordsworth begins and ends. Solitude and stone pile alike belong to the dark pattern; the landscape seems set for a tale of guilt and sorrow. And so to an extent it is, for the boy Luke, lovingly reared by his father in the lonely valley, betrays his trust when he is sent to the city to thrive in trade and make good a loss that Michael has suffered. But essentially the story is not Luke's story; the boy vanishes beyond the seas and the center of the poem lies in Michael's endurance of his sorrow.

While the valley, now that Michael and his habitation have vanished, is an utter solitude, to Michael its fields and hills were almost life itself. They had laid

> Strong hold on his affections, were to him
> A pleasurable feeling of blind love.

His love for his land was exceeded only by his love for his son, the child born to his old age, who, "Something between a hindrance and a help," had from his earliest days aided his father. Love aided love; from the boy came

> Feelings and emanations—things which were
> Light to the sun and music to the wind [7]

5. "A slumber did my spirit seal." Cleanth Brooks, in "Irony and 'Ironic' Poetry," *College English,* 9 (February, 1948), 236, finds that this poem conveys "agonized shock" at "horrible inertness," and that the final image of the rotation of the earth suggests meaningless motion, "motion that is mechanically repetitive." To my mind, the final image places the girl's inanimacy within the movement of the larger world she has joined. Cf. *The Prelude,* I, 459–60, where the cliffs wheeling by "as if the earth had rolled / With visible motion her diurnal round" are one of the manifestations of the *life* of things. Brooks is right in finding irony in the poem, but it is the irony of death-as-part-of-life.

6. Ll. 11–12.

7. Ll. 74–6, 189, 201–2.

so that Michael's land was dearer than before. From the light of the household lamp that regularly shone in the cottage as the little family worked in the evening, their dwelling was known as the Evening Star. Love and light, if not a superabundance of life, counterpoise the solitude and the stone pile.

Twice in the poem, lines 43–4 and 454–5, Wordsworth tells us that Michael's

> bodily frame had been from youth to age
> Of an unusual strength.

When the news of the boy's disgrace came back to Michael, rocklike he endured his sorrow.

> Among the rocks
> He went, and still looked up to sun and cloud,
> And listened to the wind; and, as before,
> Performed all kinds of labour for his sheep,
> And for the land, his small inheritance.

Often he went to build the fold that his sheep needed, but though he labored at it seven years the work was still unfinished when he died. Solitary he sat by the sheepfold, and many and many a day he moved no stone. Now husband and wife are dead, the cottage is gone, but the remains

> Of the unfinished Sheep-fold may be seen
> Beside the boisterous brook of Greenhead Ghyll.[8]

Wordsworth does successfully in *Michael* what he attempted less happily in *The Thorn*. The sheepfold stands as the symbol of Michael's sorrow and endurance; Michael himself in his strong old age seems akin to the rocks and sun and clouds, elemental like the sheep and land he loves. The thorn, that wretched thing overgrown like a rock with lichens, is clearly intended to stand as a comparable symbol for Martha Ray's misery. Gray and leafless, the thorn like the stone pile belongs to the wasteland group of symbols; though alive, it is a dead thing. Set against it as a life symbol is the beauteous heap of moss with its lovely colors that seems to represent nature's healing powers. Martha Ray herself, who in her scarlet cloak sits beside the thorn

> When the blue daylight's in the skies,
> And when the whirlwind's on the hill,
> Or frosty air is keen and still,[9]

belongs like Michael to the elements. Although the narrator of the poem once in the midst of storm and rain mistook her seated form for

8. Ll. 455–9, 481–2.
9. Ll. 72–4.

a jutting crag, Martha does not seem to possess Michael's silent strength, and dark and bright remain separate, failing to fuse in her person as they do in Michael's.

The Brothers is in a way almost the exact opposite of *Michael*. Both are simple tales of sorrow, but Michael's love of the land helps him endure the grief of his son's shame, whereas to Leonard the sorrow of his brother's death makes the valley he had loved "A place in which he could not bear to live." The negative symbols in *The Brothers* have less counterpoise than have those in *Michael;* through almost all the poem Leonard stands in the solitary churchyard contemplating the grave in which his brother lies, and when the priest has finally removed all doubt from his mind that it is his brother's grave, he goes back to sea, forsaking his dream of resettling in his paternal home. Though

> The thought of death sits easy on the man
> Who has been born and dies among the mountains,

though Leonard through his long absence at sea had dreamed of home, visualizing the mountains and "the forms of sheep that grazed / On verdant hills—with dwellings among trees," and shepherds clad in country gray,[1] nevertheless to him the forms of the mountains in the end are not sufficient comfort. Here, I think, life symbols are yielding to eternity symbols, and *The Brothers* perhaps relates more nearly to the later books of *The Excursion* than to the poems in which the divine life exists here and now.

Resolution and Independence like *Michael* holds a nearly perfect balance. The poem deals, of course, with a progression of moods—the blithe unthinking happiness, the blind thoughts and dim sadness, and the resolution of the fear and dejection into a mood of self-laughter and independence of mind. The landscape, as we have already observed, varies as the mood varies, from a pleasant landscape where the hare races, to a lonely place. The unifying symbol is the old man, the leech gatherer, who in his rocklike old age manifests human ability to endure. Like Michael the old man is akin to natural things, like a huge stone, motionless as a cloud, and like Michael he holds in balance the positive and negative. The negative elements include not only the poet's dejection but the old man's wandering about the weary moors; out of that very vision of the old man's wandering comes the influx of strength.[2]

The short poems *To a Highland Girl, Glen Almain, Stepping Westward,* and *The Solitary Reaper* all have stronger elements of light and life than of darkness and loneliness. *To a Highland Girl* has perhaps least of the negative pattern: the loneliness of the spot is utterly outweighed

---

1. Ll. 426, 182-3, 62-4.
2. Further discussion of this poem will be found in the chapter dealing with the people who appear in the Wordsworthian landscape.

by the girl's heavenly brightness. Seen in the common light of day she is a dream vision, in her glad freedom reminding the poet of

> birds of tempest-loving kind—
> Thus beating up against the wind [3]

and seeming the living spirit of the lonely place. In *Glen Almain*, the narrow glen where the grave of Ossian is rumored to be, Wordsworth describes another lonely spot. No living creature illuminates this place; its rest is so deep that even a hermit's cell would violate it.

> It is not quiet, is not ease;
> But something deeper far than these:
> The separation that is here
> Is of the grave.[4]

The note of irony, that Ossian who sang of battles should sleep in such a still place, is kept subdued, but the liveliness of Ossian's themes sounds a countertheme to the deathly quiet of the narrow glen. *Stepping Westward* develops from stanza to stanza the image of the glowing sky so that the journey into death becomes a journey into radiance. Behind the traveler the land is dark, but ahead is the region bright, the journey that is endless. Moreover, though the travelers are strangers far from home, the voice of the woman who asked *"What, you are stepping westward?"* lends human sweetness to the eternal journey. Here once again the life and light pattern is moving toward an eternity pattern, but thought of eternity does not here deaden the present. More than any of the others *The Solitary Reaper* seems perfectly to fuse a sense of the dark and melancholy with a thrilling sense of overflowing life. The girl's melancholy song floods the lonely valley; encountering such a song in such a place is comparable to coming on a nightingale singing in an oasis in an Arabian desert or hearing the first cuckoo announce the coming of spring in the farthest Hebrides. Both comparisons are built on the intense excitement of song announcing the end of hardship and desolation; indirectly the effect is that the song continues to overflow, spreading to the far ends of the earth. And as the poet questions whether the plaintive numbers tell of old, unhappy, far-off things or of some natural sorrow that may come again in the future, the song spreads in time too, becoming the music of humanity across time.[5] Song and sorrow are one, and song rises into the solitude, flooding and filling it.

3. Ll. 45–6.
4. Ll. 25–8.
5. See Wimsatt, "The Structure of the 'Concrete Universal' in Literature," *PMLA, 62* (March, 1947), 274–5, and Frederick A. Pottle, "The Eye and the Object in the Poetry of Wordsworth," in *Wordsworth: Centenary Studies Presented at Cornell and Princeton Universities,* ed. Dunklin, pp. 40–1.

The first book of *The Excursion* should perhaps be included among the poems in which Wordsworth holds the two patterns together; certainly he attempted a reconciliation for the sorrow and despair of Margaret's story. Here as in *Guilt and Sorrow* Wordsworth's focus shifted as he worked on the poem: the earliest passages, apparently dating from 1795, were concerned solely with the story of Margaret whose husband was driven by unemployment to enlist.[6] Passages in MS A describing the ruined cottage correspond closely to lines of *Incipient Madness*, a poem included among the *juvenilia*, in which the unnamed woman's mind is described as being "Sick and extravagant,"

> driven to that state
> In which all past experience melts away,
> And the rebellious heart to its own will
> Fashions the laws of nature.[7]

The Margaret of *The Ruined Cottage* is not rebellious but suffers the long grief of her husband's absence like one

> By sorrow laid asleep; . . .
> A human being destined to awake
> To human life, or something very near
> To human life, when he shall come again
> For whom she suffered.[8]

Apparently in the first version the Pedlar who relates Margaret's story was a stranger to the Poet,[9] but the Pedlar's function, like that of the sailor in *Guilt and Sorrow*, grew so that in MS B, written during the winter and spring of 1797–98,[1] "The Pedlar's character . . . makes a very, certainly the *most*, considerable part of the Poem."[2] Nevertheless the poem was still being called *The Ruined Cottage;* not until December, 1801–March, 1802, does Dorothy Wordsworth in her journal refer to the poem as *The Pedlar*. As late as March 10, 1802, her journal shows that Wordsworth still regarded *The Pedlar* as an independent poem and was talking about publishing it along with *Peter Bell*.[3] The date at which Wordsworth ceased to regard it as a separate poem is not

6. According to Wordsworth, the lines first written were those beginning "Nine tedious years" and ending "last human tenant of these ruined walls," *The Excursion*, I, 871–916. But Darbishire dates from *ca.* 1795 MS A which has "the central part of Margaret's story, the unhappy events leading to her husband's breakdown," *The Excursion*, I, 502–70, 582–91. *PW, 5*, 369.

7. *PW, 1*, 316, ll. 61–5. See *1*, 314–16, 375; *5*, 377.

8. *The Excursion*, I, 786–90.

9. See *Unpublished Letters of Samuel Taylor Coleridge*, ed. Earl Leslie Griggs (London, Constable, 1932), *1*, 76–7.

1. *PW, 5*, 378.

2. Dorothy Wordsworth to Mary Hutchinson, March 5, 1798, *EL*, p. 176.

3. *Journals of Dorothy Wordsworth*, ed. Ernest de Selincourt (London, Macmillan, 1941), *1*, 92–119, 122.

known, but by the end of 1804 he was speaking of it as part of *The Recluse*.[4] Even in MS B, however, the tale is one of unrelieved suffering as Margaret waits year after year for her husband, who does not return, and sinks deeper and deeper into sorrow. The slow decay of cottage and garden are the visible evidence of the encroachment of poverty and grief; eventually she lives exposed to wind and rain

> Even at the side of her own fire. Yet still
> She loved this wretched spot, nor would for worlds
> Have parted hence; and still that length of road,
> And this rude bench, one torturing hope endeared,
> Fast rooted at her heart: and here, my Friend,—
> In sickness she remained; and here she died;
> Last human tenant of these ruined walls![5]

So the story originally ended. The development of the character of the Pedlar—now called the Wanderer—resulted not only in the aesthetic distancing of Margaret's story but in the framing of it by the Wanderer's philosophic mind. The extent to which Wordsworth succeeded in combining the bleak symbols with the reconciling ideas is perhaps a question: there seems nothing quite comparable to Michael's stone pile where strength and desolation meet. The desolation was Margaret's; the strength is the Wanderer's; and to my mind the reconciliation is incomplete. The weeds that have overrun house and garden become in the end the reconciling symbol: seen with an unworthy eye the rank spear grass and the nettles are signs of desolation and decay, but to the Wanderer's eye the weeds and the grass silvered over by mist and rain convey tranquillity. Evidently Wordsworth himself was not altogether satisfied with his symbol for in 1845 he added lines 934–40 and 952–5, turning the reader to the cross and to "the breast of Faith." I am myself inclined to see in the use of the spear grass as a reconciling symbol the key to Wordsworth's later degeneration: the life of nature may take Margaret to itself and soften the desolation, but the pain and sorrow and despair of her life are not thereby altered. Only the painful memory is altered, and the alteration of the memory seems an evasion.[6]

The reconciling symbol of *The White Doe* seems to me equally open to question. Suffering, says Wordsworth, "is permanent, obscure and dark, / And has the nature of infinity." The "gracious openings" which lie "through that darkness" may release the soul from mortal bonds until it rises "Even to the fountain-head of peace divine."[7] The darkness

---

4. See *PW*, 5, 366, 369–70, 409–10.
5. *The Excursion*, 1, 910–16.
6. See below, pp. 105–6.
7. Lines first used as a motto to the poem in 1837: the first six are from *The Borderers*, ll. 1539–44, spoken by Oswald.

of Emily Norton's suffering is beyond question. Her father and eight
of her nine brothers join the ill-fated rising of the North in support of
Percy and Neville; in the defeat of the North all are put to death. The
eldest brother Francis, like Emily a Protestant and unwilling to rebel,
perishes solely because he attempts to fulfill his father's last request that
the banner which the rebelling Nortons carried into battle be returned
to Bolton Priory. Emily, as Francis foresaw, is left alone, "The last
leaf on a blasted tree," to suffer the shock.

> Her only unextinguished light;
> Her last companion in a dearth
> Of love, upon a hopeless earth [8]

is the white doe, from which the poem takes its name.

In the figure of the doe Wordsworth seems to be attempting a symbol that will unite the healing power of nature with that of spiritual grace.
From the moment of its first appearance the white doe is more than
natural. Into the Sabbath day scene, hushed and quiet as the people
worship among the ruins of Bolton Priory,

> Comes gliding in with lovely gleam,
> Comes gliding in serene and slow,
> Soft and silent as a dream,
> A solitary Doe!

White as a lily, beauteous as the moon in a cloudless sky or a single
ship glittering in sunlight, the doe is so bright that it is uncertain whether
she is truly a forest creature

> Or a Spirit for one day given,
> A pledge of grace from purest heaven.

Wandering through the ruined priory the doe makes a glory in the
gloom; reappearing in the sunlight, she sheds on the flowers "A more
than sunny liveliness." A radiant creature, who seems a votary or pilgrim,[9] the doe is so successfully spiritualized, so apart from her own
kind, that she seems unreal. The weeds and spear grass of *The Ruined
Cottage* may fail to persuade one of the unreality of Margaret's suffering but they are convincing as weeds and spear grass. The white doe
is less convincing as doe.

Furthermore, the weeds are a natural symbol both of desolation
and decay and of the life of nature. The white doe in its white radiance
is a symbol of eternity; it moves among the "despoil and desolation"
that have settled upon Rylstone after the death of the Norton men, but
it has so little animality that it seems supernatural more than natural.

8. Ll. 567, 343–5.
9. Ll. 55–66, 77–8, 92, 105, 108, 110.

White as foam, white as whitest cloud on high, silver bright, like a patch of April snow,[1] the doe seems almost a disembodied presence.[2] Bringing to Emily associations [3] that are a source of both pain and comfort, she combines the healing powers of nature and of memory in addition to seeming emblematic of the pure spirituality to which Emily attains. Like the landscape in *Tintern Abbey* the white doe is idealized so that the natural rises into the spiritual, so that the natural *is* spiritual. Unlike the landscape, however, the doe is never really natural. One suspects that in Wordsworth's mind the doe and Emily were sisters, united not merely by association but in deeper spiritual unity, both children of the Eternal. Emily's anguish is allayed

> by sympathies
> Aloft ascending, and descending deep,
> Even to the inferior Kinds.[4]

To an extent too the doe seems intended to be, like the Highland girl, the spirit of the place. But again her overspiritualization makes her seem an arbitrary, not a natural, symbol.

The light and life pattern seems in this poem to be splitting apart—light is separating from life. Emily masters her suffering largely by withdrawal from life:

> By sorrow lifted towards her God;
> Uplifted to the purest sky
> Of undisturbed mortality.

She remains "apart from human cares" and "to the world returned no more";

> At length, thus faintly, faintly tied
> To earth, she was set free, and died.

The white doe who survives her likewise is " 'not a Child of Time, / But Daughter of the Eternal Prime!' " Desolation and light exist together in this poem; the white doe alters Emily's melancholy from "stern and rigorous" to "Mild, and grateful,"

> Not sunless gloom or unenlightened,
> But by tender fancies brightened.[5]

But while grief is conquered, the affirmation is hardly an affirmation of this life.

Had Wordsworth been able to hold together in one vision the dark

1. Ll. 1568, 1806, 1741, 1647, 1003.
2. She is called a "Presence" in l. 1744.
3. Ll. 1674–9.
4. Dedication, ll. 43–5.
5. Ll. 1851–3, 1859–60, 1864–5, 1909–10, 1597, 1758–60.

vision of the burden of suffering and the bright vision of redeeming love, he would, I think, have written the great philosophic poem that he wished to write. The splitting of the image patterns which amounted to a rejection of life rose perhaps simply from a failure of vital energies. Whatever its cause, the results are clear. Life and light and love departed from this actual world and at the same time from Wordsworth's poetry.

IV

People

THROUGH the Wordsworthian landscape move the Wordsworthian figures, the most memorable of them almost emanations of the landscape itself. Elemental and enduring, suffering and solitary—there are clearly recognizable figures who recur and recur. Yet they are difficult if not impossible to discuss without much overlapping. Somewhat arbitrarily I have isolated the figures of the child, the young girl, the joyous irresponsible, the suffering woman, the enduring old man. Some of these figures—young girl, suffering woman, old man—are frequently also solitaries; some of them are also wanderers. The solitary and wanderer I have therefore left for separate discussion at the end of this chapter. Once again it may be illuminating to follow Wordsworth chronologically within the groupings, watching the figures emerge and the patterns cross and develop.

The figure of the child does not appear significantly either in Wordsworth's *juvenilia* or in his early poetry, and it vanishes as a real interest after 1807. In the period 1798–1807, however, Wordsworth's interest in the child seems threefold. Primarily there is the figure who belonged to memory, the child William;[1] then there are actual children whose psychology interested Wordsworth;[2] most important, there is the life of the spirit for which the child is a supreme symbol. Before 1798 there is only the little child whose father is mercilessly beating it in *Guilt and Sorrow*. As an image of undeserved suffering the child fails to develop; undeserved suffering in Wordsworth centers round the female of the species. As an agent of redemption, however, the child persists. To a certain extent Wordsworth's introspective interest in William is in just this. Uncertain of his powers, unable to write the great poem he wished to write, Wordsworth turned to memory in an effort to regain the hiding places of his power, the wellsprings of his being.[3] Interest in the boy William overlaps with interest in the child as symbol of indwelling life: the boy William was to the man Wordsworth the way back into creative power.

The passages in *The Prelude* which refer most directly to childhood

---

1. See Charles Williams, "The Analysis of William," in *Reason and Beauty in the Poetic Mind* (Oxford, Clarendon Press, 1933), pp. 17–29.

2. See *Anecdote for Fathers, To H. C. Six Years Old, Characteristics of a Child Three Years Old.*

3. *The Prelude*, I, 237–69.

as such refer to the child's creative mind. Speaking of his—or William's
—early love of reading and its strengthening of imaginative life, Wordsworth remarks,

> Dumb yearnings, hidden appetites, are ours,
> And *they must* have their food. Our childhood sits,
> Our simple childhood, sits upon a throne
> That hath more power than all the elements.
> I guess not what this tells of Being past,
> Nor what it augurs of the life to come.

Here the throne of childhood seems to refer to the strength of the
inner creative life; the individual has not yet learned to live

> In reconcilement with our stinted powers;
> To endure this state of meagre vassalage.[4]

Later, remembering the spots of time in which the sense of imaginative
power had been most clearly his, he writes,

> Oh! mystery of man, from what a depth
> Proceed thy honours. I am lost, but see
> In simple childhood something of the base
> On which thy greatness stands; but this I feel,
> That from thyself it comes, that thou must give,
> Else never canst receive. The days gone by
> Return upon me almost from the dawn
> Of life: the hiding-places of man's power
> Open; I would approach them, but they close.[5]

The child is father of the man; creative power depends on the ability
to keep open the roads that lead back to childhood.[6]

It is perhaps significant that lines 232–65 of Book II of *The Prelude,*
the passage in which the infant babe, responsive to his mother's love, is
seen as possessing the "first / Poetic spirit of our human life," are connected by Leavis with *Tintern Abbey* and by Lionel Trilling with the
Intimations ode. According to Leavis, Wordsworth in *The Prelude*
passage "is explaining how he comes to have the kind of experience he
describes in *Tintern Abbey*;[7] Trilling finds that "the first affections"

4. v, 506–11, 517–18.
5. xii, 272–80.
6. See W. R. Niblett's comment in "Wordsworth's Study of Childhood," *The London
Quarterly and Holborn Review, 169* (1944), 49, "The child is father of the man not
merely chronologically but at every instant. For in the sensitiveness and humility of
childhood and childlikeness is the source of creative awareness and power. . . . the man
separated from any return to the infinite child in him is separated from the springs of
his own being."
7. "Wordsworth," in *Revaluation: Tradition and Development in English Poetry,*
pp. 161–2.

for which the poet gives thanks in the ode are the affections that lead the child to perceive objects not merely as objects but "as objects-and-judgments, as valued objects," to perceive "in short, with 'glory.' " [8] Both critics have evidently recognized in the child Wordsworth's image for the creative life of the mind.

Yet the child remains baffling and elusive, part symbol, part reality. The fundamental difficulty of the great *Intimations* ode seems to me to have its source here. As we have already observed, the opening and closing passages of the poem which deal with landscape move on only one level: the celestial light is gone. This light, however, serves as a transitional symbol leading to the central symbol of the poem, the child, and the child is at once a natural child and a symbol. At one and the same time Wordsworth traces the growth of man, with the attendant loss of the freshness of the world, and employs the child as a symbol of immanent divinity. In *Tintern Abbey* the landscape by virtue of its unchanging and enfolding quality symbolizes the living presence of the divine. The child is a more difficult symbol: it is not so easy to distinguish the physical child who becomes a man from the spiritual child, symbol of the soul. [9]

The problem as it is presented in the ode is that of keeping any of the life of the spirit alive, to keep it from being utterly deadened by the pressure of the natural world. Stanza v, in which Wordsworth introduces his central image, shifting from the personal "I" of the opening and closing sections of the poem to the more philosophical and generalized "we" of the center, opens with a semicontradiction: to the extent that our birth is a sleep and a forgetting, we are leaving spiritual reality when we enter this world; to the extent that the soul rises with us, our life's star, we bring spiritual reality with us into this world. The light that once irradiated the landscape came from the pristine soul; as the

8. Lionel Trilling, "The Immortality Ode," in *The Liberal Imagination: Essays in Literature and Society* (New York, Viking Press, 1950), pp. 145–6.

9. For interpretations of the ode differing from mine the reader should consult Arthur Beatty, *William Wordsworth: His Doctrine and Art in Their Historical Relations,* University of Wisconsin Studies in Language and Literature, No. 24 (Madison, University of Wisconsin Press, 1927), pp. 81–9; Brooks, "Wordsworth and the Paradox of the Imagination," *The Well Wrought Urn,* pp. 114–38; C. M. Bowra, "Ode on Intimations of Immortality," in *The Romantic Imagination* (Cambridge, Harvard University Press, 1949), pp. 76–102; and Trilling, "The Immortality Ode," pp. 129–59.

Beatty sees the structure of the poem as I do, finding that stanzas I–IV and IX–XI form "a self-consistent poem founded solely on the three ages, and stanzas V–IX a complete intercalary poem on the glory of the child and his derivation from afar." In his opinion, however, the central theme of the poem is "the justification of hope and the triumph of life in the coming of maturity," and the child symbol of the central section simply confusing and misleading. Brooks finds stanza VII weak and the conclusion of the poem insufficiently dramatized. Bowra sees the poem as dealing with crisis, explanation, and consolation; Trilling sees the structure as dividing at the end of stanza IV, with stanzas V–VIII giving negative resistance to growth and stanzas IX–XI positive acceptance of growth. The ode is in his opinion "largely naturalistic in its intention."

youth matures and turns increasingly from his inner life out into the world (who daily farther from the east / Must travel), the vision fades into the light of common day. Stanza VI converts the whole material world into a maternal figure (Earth fills her lap) and all adults, occupied with the pleasures of this earth, into children who foolishly forget their real treasure. Thus even while dealing with normal growth and development Wordsworth holds the child image steadily before us and with the word "glories" (Forget the glories he hath known) continues the light that envelops it. Stanza VII, sometimes regarded as superfluous, is devoted to renewing the image of the actual child, now brightened by the light from his father's eyes. Quietly the concluding lines

> As if his whole vocation
> Were endless imitation

remind us that the child has another and more real vocation—the spiritual. This stanza creates the image of the living, playing child so firmly that Wordsworth is able in the next stanza to develop the child symbol without losing contact with reality. Here, at the heart of the poem, the little child is at once the little child who all too soon will extinguish the divine spark under the freight of earthly things and the little child who shall lead us into the kingdom. In his soul's immensity the little child lives in his own world, not yet yoked by custom and tradition.[1] Still possessing his heritage, the soul that rises with us, he possesses intuitive knowledge of truths that the adults he lives among have long lost sight of and must struggle to regain. The little cottage girl of *We Are Seven* and the Dear Child of "It is a beauteous evening" both are specific examples of Wordsworth's statements here: the cottage child sings with complete confidence to her brother and sister who lie in the graveyard; young Caroline can play happily without solemn thought, her nature being innately divine. The lines of stanza VIII which Coleridge criticized as grandiose have been ably defended;[2] really they should need no defense. Set against the darkness in which the adults have lost their knowledge of spiritual truths, the darkness of the grave, the little child stands glorious on his being's height. Immortality broods over him like the arching sky,[3] visible as a presence.

The central paradox of the ode is that Wordsworth does what he says he no longer can do: surely the image of the child appears in vision-

---

1. Cf. *The Prelude*, III, 144–5. See also *Maternal Grief* where all the children are vouchsafed "Reflected beams of . . . celestial light."

2. See I. A. Richards, *Coleridge on Imagination* (New York, Harcourt, Brace, 1935), pp. 133–7; G. Wilson Knight, "The Wordsworthian Profundity," in *The Starlit Dome*, pp. 44–8; Brooks, "Wordsworth and the Paradox of the Imagination," *The Well Wrought Urn*, pp. 129–36.

3. Cf. "The gentleness of heaven broods o'er the Sea," l. 5 in "It is a beauteous evening, calm and free."

ary light. But the image is only briefly sustained, for the natural child triumphs over the child symbol of indwelling spirit. The stated irony is that the little child hastens so blindly into the blind word of adults; [4] the real irony is that the symbolic child, who should be ageless and timeless, is asked why he grows up. This disappearance of central symbol in the natural creature accounts, I think, for the dissatisfaction that so many readers have felt with the end of the ode. But mystic vision is seldom sustained long. The visionary height is the center of the poem; as in *Tintern Abbey,* so here Wordsworth leads the reader down from the height to leave him back in literal reality. G. Wilson Knight comments, "We must see the ode spatially, not merely temporally: that is, must view its pattern simultaneously outrolled, the beginning and end of framework, the outer rose-petals, the centre its fiery heart, wherein we have our vision of the child, transfigured by poetry." [5] The question remains, however, whether the outer framework and the inner vision cohere. Landscape provides a symbol of the divine in *Tintern Abbey* and remains landscape; the child provides a symbol of the divine in the ode, but first and last has vanished in "an eye / That hath kept watch o'er man's mortality." Wordsworth's reconciling idea is simply that the divine spark never completely dies: [6] we live aware of worlds not realized; we remember, even if dimly, moments that belong to eternity. Hence even in the middle of the journey of life

> Our Souls have sight of that immortal sea
>   Which brought us hither,
>   Can in a moment travel thither,
> And see the Children sport upon the shore,
> And hear the mighty waters rolling evermore. [7]

Hence the adult mind is reconciled to itself: the heart of the poem is the vision of the divine child, and in the heart of the man the child still lives. [8]

The fact that the Solitary of *The Excursion* when first encountered

4. See Brooks, "Wordsworth and the Paradox of the Imagination," *The Well Wrought Urn,* p. 123.

5. "The Wordsworthian Profundity," in *The Starlit Dome,* p. 48.

6. Cf. *The Excursion,* iv, where the Wanderer tells how his "Particle divine remained unquenched"; though the frost of age gathers round his heart, the divine flowers still bloom (ll. 51–6). The wanderer asserts his faith, but

> Alas! the endowment of immortal power
> Is matched unequally with custom, time,
> And domineering faculties of sense
> In *all.*

7. Ll. 162–8. Wimsatt comments on the structure of this image in "The Structure of Romantic Nature Imagery," in *The Age of Johnson, Essays Presented to Chauncey Brewster Tinker,* p. 302, that the children appear in the vehicle by attraction from the tenor. I suspect that part of the attraction comes from the main vehicle of the poem—the child who reveals the divine life.

8. See *Peter Bell,* l. 969, where Peter at the moment of his transformation becomes weak and helpless "as an infant child."

is comforting a child looks as if Wordsworth had contemplated a further development of the child as instrument of redemption. Wordsworth's note that he had intended to have the Solitary witness "some religious ceremony—a sacrament, say, in the open fields, or a preaching among the mountains—which, by recalling to his mind the days of his early childhood . . . might have dissolved his heart into tenderness" [9] confirms this appearance. The child who lives in the heart was apparently to open the way to spiritual rebirth—once again the child is part actual, part memory, part symbol.

The second figure, the young girl, appears to a limited extent in both Wordsworth's very early and his late poetry, but like the image of the child it appears most prominently in the poetry of 1798–1807. We have already observed that in two of the *juvenilia,* the *Anacreon* and *Beauty and Moonlight,* landscape imagery is used to describe the person of the poet's beloved. This connection between the landscape and the young girl persisted, so that Wordsworth's loveliest girls are nature's children, almost embodiments of the landscape. Even Idonea, Marmaduke's beloved in *The Borderers,* who has little enough of life about her, is described as reared "By lowly nature." [1] The point does not need to be labored: Lucy, the Highland girl, and the solitary reaper have already been discussed in connection with the landscape. Lucy Gray, the solitary child who was

> —The sweetest thing that ever grew
> Beside a human door!

belongs to the lonesome wild in much the same way that the Highland girl belongs to the lake, the bay, the waterfall. She is the spirit of that solitary moor and still trips across it, singing her "solitary song / That whistles in the wind." The landscape poem "It was an April morning," in which Wordsworth named the joyous dell for his sister, simply carries this feeling for a person as the spirit of a place one step further.

The poem "She was a Phantom of delight," which developed from verses written as part of *To a Highland Girl* to become a description of Mary Wordsworth,[2] separates the image of the girl from any particular scene. The girl's attributes are still those of natural things (Her eyes as stars of Twilight fair, etc.) but the spirit of nature has become a woman,

> A Creature not too bright or good
> For human nature's daily food;

and in the end the term "spirit" is given added depth. The traveler between life and death carries about her "something of angelic light." *The*

9. *IF.*
1. Act v, l. 2334.
2. *IF.*

Three Cottage Girls, written as one of the memorials of the tour on the continent in 1820, once again pays tribute to the Highland girl. These girls, though each is given a local habitation—one Italian, one Helvetian, one Highland—are less vivid images of the flowering of life. The Italian maid glitters like a star; the Helvetian's beauty "dazzles the thick wood"; [3] but only the Highland girl really seems a "Bright Spirit." Lines 59–71, added to the poem in 1837, dim the image of her brightness, questioning whether time has not presumably brought grief and distress to her. But the concluding lines

> Time cannot thin thy flowing hair,
> Nor take one ray of light from Thee;
> For in my Fancy thou dost share
> The gift of immortality;

are almost worthy of Wordsworth's original vision of the "Bright Spirit." *The Triad,* written in 1828, praises Edith Southey, Dora Wordsworth, and Sara Coleridge as "Bright Beings" but invokes them as "Mere Mortals, bodied forth in vision." [4] One by one the three girls are praised as possible brides—Edith with regal imagery, Dora as nature's child, and Sara with imagery from the skies—in a highly artificial arrangement.

Child and young girl are both figures of life, belonging to the landscape of love and light and joy. The third figure, the joyous irresponsible—who is perhaps less a recurrent figure than a convenient grouping—likewise seems the product of Wordsworth's mighty affirmation of life. The joyous irresponsibles too belong to the period 1798–1807, though publication of *The Waggoner* was delayed until 1819. Idiot boy, beggars, thieves, idle shepherd boys, drunken waggoner—Wordsworth for a time delighted in any manifestation of the joy of living, however lowly. Wordsworth's intention in *The Idiot Boy* may have been to trace "the maternal passion"; [5] what wells up through the poem is the idiot boy's delight in his nocturnal excursion. When the pony moved, the boy was so delighted that he could not hold the bridle and "quite forgot his holly whip." [6] With his lips burring merrily, off he went on high and wonderful adventures—perhaps

> To lay his hands upon a star,
> And in his pocket bring it home;

perhaps to go galloping "with head and heels on fire." Wordsworth himself seems intoxicated by Johnny's mindless pleasure as he protests

3. L. 40.
4. L. 12.
5. "Preface to the Lyrical Ballads," *PW, 2,* 388, n.
6. L. 84.

to the Muses against his inability to relate "But half of what to him be-
fell." [7] The old Cumberland beggar who plies his weary journey "Bow-
bent, his eyes for ever on the ground" is, of course, scarcely a manifestation of either life or joy. Yet he too is part of the

> spirit and pulse of good,
> A life and soul, to every mode of being
> Inseparably linked. [8]

He at least stirs others to acts ot love and gives the poorest poor oppor-
tunity to show kindness. The other beggars, the imposing woman like
an Amazonian queen and the rascally boys with the flowers around their
hats, clearly delight the poet by their physical beauty and irrepressible
activity. They may be weeds, but they are weeds "of glorious feature." [9]
The idle shepherd boys who nearly lose a lamb because of their joyous
carelessness, the pilfering old man and his. little grandson [1]—the poet
loves them and hates only Andrew Jones, who took a penny from a poor
cripple. [2] The waggoner who despite his weakness for drink can manage
his horses while others cannot, whose unquestioning kindness to the
sailor's wife leads to his comradeship with the sailor and thus to his
destruction, is termed without qualification

> Benjamin the good,
> The patient, and the tender-hearted. [3]

If child, young girl, and joyous irresponsible are all life symbols, the
fourth figure, the suffering woman, belongs primarily to the dark landscape. [4] This figure in its earliest form is one of undeserved suffering
and innocence; as the pattern develops, some of the women suffer the
shame of bearing illegitimate children; some simply endure their suffering, some break under suffering, and some are purified by it.

The Female Vagrant, Margaret of *The Ruined Cottage,* Idonea of
The Borderers suffer woes not of their own making. Undoubtedly
Wordsworth's adherence to Godwinism was responsible for the extent
to which the plague of war and the injustice of social conditions afflict

7. Ll. 320–1, 332, 340.
8. Ll. 52, 77–9.
9. *Beggars,* l. 18.
1. *The Idle Shepherd-Boys, The Two Thieves.* See also *The Farmer of Tilsbury Vale,*
in which the joyous irresponsibility of the farmer is dimmed by homesickness.
2. *Andrew Jones.*
3. *The Waggoner,* iv, 182–3.
4. Those who are inclined to see in this figure simply the result of Wordsworth's experience with Annette Vallon in 1792 should be given pause by the presence of the suffering woman in two of the *juvenilia, A Ballad,* dated 1787, and No. xvi, which reads like
an early draft of *The Female Vagrant* and which De Selincourt tentatively dates 1791.
Interestingly enough, the deserted girl of *A Ballad* is named Mary; her lover is named
William. No one has yet suggested an early lover's quarrel between Wordsworth and
Mary Hutchinson!

Margaret and the Female Vagrant. It can hardly be held responsible for the curious passivity with which these women suffer. The Female Vagrant's life showed normal activity until the deaths of her husband and children occurred; thereafter she was helplessly adrift, "hopeless, as if cast on some bare rock." She describes herself as unfit for toil or service, brooding over her griefs,

> My deep-drawn sighs no effort could confine;
> In open air forgetful would I sit
> Whole hours, with idle arms in moping sorrow knit.[5]

Margaret likewise withdraws from life under the unhappiness of her husband's enlistment. She neglects her infant child; her eyelids droop, her whole body is subdued.

> In every act
> Pertaining to her house-affairs, appeared
> The careless stillness of a thinking soul
> Self-occupied; to which all outward things
> Are like an idle matter.[6]

Her heart remains tied to the "dead things," [7] her husband's idle loom, his Sunday garments "hung / Upon the self-same nail; his very staff" behind the door. "Reckless and alone," she sustains to her death the torturing hope of seeing her husband return. In neither case is there any implication that the woman could in any way have remedied herself. Margaret's was "A sore heart-wasting"; [8] the Female Vagrant's spirit remains under its perpetual weight. Their suffering is "permanent, obscure and dark, / And has the nature of infinity." Through their darkness no gracious openings lie.

Ruth and Emily Norton are further figures of completely innocent sufferers, though for them the darkness is in differing degrees relieved. Ruth's trouble is deep rooted, having its origin in her neglected childhood. But in her childhood she had run free over hill and dale, piping on her pipe of straw,

> Had built a bower upon the green,
> As if she from her birth had been
> An infant of the woods.[9]

When the gay, handsome youth from Georgia deserts her after their marriage, she goes mad, but even in her illness

> Yet sometimes milder hours she knew,
> Nor wanted sun, nor rain, nor dew,

5. *Guilt and Sorrow*, ll. 371, 423, 429, 430–2.
6. *The Excursion*, I, 736, 792, 795–9.
7. See *Incipient Madness, PW*, I, 316, l. 55.
8. *The Excursion*, I, 851–4, 905, 875.
9. *Ruth*, ll. 10–12.

Nor pastimes of the May;
—They all were with her in her cell;
And a clear brook with cheerful knell
Did o'er the pebbles play.

Eventually she escapes from her prison and returns to the fields and woods that in her childhood had almost been her home. In what is virtually a second childhood

She sleeps beneath the greenwood tree,
And other home hath none.[1]

Ruth breaks under suffering, but her regression to her childhood ways mitigates her suffering as the suffering of the Female Vagrant or of Margaret is never mitigated. The mad carousing of the cup of wrong gives way to the music of Ruth's hemlock flute and the childish play with little water mills. While her body, exposed to "damp, and rain, and cold," must suffer, at least the "master-current of her brain" runs free.[2]

If the Female Vagrant and Margaret seem to withdraw from active life into an infinity of suffering, if Ruth withdraws into infantilism, Emily Norton withdraws into religion. Alice P. Comparetti defends Emily, maintaining that her "state is not passive as opposed to active, but contemplative as opposed to active; hers is a very active victory achieved in the world of spirit." The important thing, she thinks, "is not Emily's retreat, but her life of contemplation, which must be pursued in solitude . . . so that the reader may perceive the supreme power of faith alone." [3] The difficulty with this defense is that, as we have previously observed, Emily's ascent from distress and trouble is not really into a sanctity that is fuller life but is a withdrawal. Francis foresees his sister's destiny:

"A Soul, by force of sorrows high,
Uplifted to the purest sky
Of undisturbed humanity!" [4]

When we first see Emily after the death of father and brothers, she already is carrying "inward a serene / And perfect sway," her grief subjected to a holy "Though stern and rigorous, melancholy!" After the white doe has reappeared to share Emily's solitude, Emily's gloom is lightened so that she is "Forlorn, but not disconsolate" and able to return from "the abyss . . . Of thought" without grief or pain.[5] Stoicism

1. *Ruth*, ll. 199–204, 227–8.
2. L. 211 to end.
3. Alice P. Comparetti, ed., *The White Doe of Rylstone*, Cornell Studies in English, 29 (Ithaca, Cornell University Press, 1940), 9, 14.
4. *The White Doe of Rylstone*, ll. 585–7.
5. Ll. 1593–4, 1597, 1820 ff.

is here, as Jane Worthington Smyser has observed, tempered with tenderness.[6] But the renewal of feeling binds Emily only to past memories and to supernatural grace. Emily's triumph over pain and grief leaves her "faintly, faintly tied / To earth"; her heart like Margaret's remains with dead things.[7]

The Female Vagrant, Margaret, Ruth, and Emily Norton are all essentially solitary figures. The figure of woman and child follows much the same development from unrelieved suffering to suffering tempered by religion. The unhappy woman of *An Evening Walk,* the Grison gypsy of *Descriptive Sketches,* Martha Ray of *The Thorn,* the mad mother of *Her Eyes Are Wild*—all are figures of suffering that has the nature of infinity.[8] Their stories can be summed up in the doleful cry that Martha cries at all times and seasons:

"Oh misery! oh misery!
Oh woe is me! oh misery!" [9]

But the story of Ellen in *The Excursion,* while equally unhappy, is a story to which "religious tenderness of heart, / Grieving for sin" lends sanctity. Described as a weeping and rueful Magdalene, Ellen mourned her own transgression with such sincere penitence that the Pastor describes her as "Meek Saint! through patience glorified on earth!" In her

The ghastly face of cold decay put on
A sun-like beauty, and appeared divine!

Enduring her suffering without complaint,

through the cloud of death, her Spirit passed
Into that pure and unknown world of love.[1]

The figure of the deserted woman is linked to the purely maternal figure by the brief poem *The Forsaken,* which printed alone reads as a woman's plea for her lover's return but which was an overflow from *The Affliction of Margaret———.*[2] Once again the development that we have observed from bleak unrelieved suffering to suffering relieved by religion

6. Jane Worthington [Smyser], *Wordsworth's Reading in Roman Prose* (New Haven, Yale University Press, 1946), 70.
7. *The White Doe,* ll. 1864–5. The *Lament of Mary Queen of Scots* (1817) continues this figure in the late poetry. Here the unhappy queen turns to the cross for support. Both the sonnets *Captivity.—Mary Queen of Scots* (published 1818) and *Mary Queen of Scots Landing at the Mouth of the Derwent, Workington* (1833), however, are close to the early poems in their picture of unrelieved suffering.
8. See lines prefatory to *The White Doe.*
9. *The Thorn,* ll. 65–6, 76–7, 191, 198, 241–2.
1. VI, 798–9, 814, 987, 1034, 1036–7, 1049–50. Julia of *Vaudracour and Julia* cannot be included among these figures. The story is so much Vaudracour's that he seems to be the suffering figure there.
2. *IF.*

holds good, as a glance at the following titles reveals: *The Complaint of a Forsaken Indian Woman, The Sailor's Mother, The Emigrant Mother, The Affliction of Margaret* ———, and *The Force of Prayer.*[3] The noblest of these poems is *The Affliction of Margaret* ———, in which a mother who has had no news of her son in seven years voices her sense of dark uncertainty:

> Perhaps some dungeon hears thee groan,
> Maimed, mangled by inhuman men;
> Or thou upon a desert thrown
> Inheritest the lion's den;
> Or hast been summoned to the deep,
> Thou, thou and all thy mates, to keep
> An incommunicable sleep.[4]

The sailor's mother, who knows that her son is dead, does not suffer this dreadful uncertainty; she has his bird to cherish. The emigrant mother is partially comforted and partially tortured by the child that is not her own. Real relief from suffering comes in *The Force of Prayer,* which begins with what seems another incurable sorrow.

> *"What is good for a bootless bene?"*
> With these dark words begins my Tale;
> And their meaning is, whence can comfort spring
> When Prayer is of no avail?

But prayer is not unavailing: the Lady Aäliza built Bolton Priory in memory of her dead son [5] and in time found succor and "a patience to her grief." Here the endlessness of suffering is denied:

> Oh! there is never sorrow of heart
> That shall lack a timely end,
> If but to God we turn, and ask
> Of Him to be our friend! [6]

The Widow on Windermere Side, written as late as 1837, is a picture in which religious consolation and insane grief are almost one. The mother's reason gives way to visions of her son who seems to her an angel,

> and in earthly ecstasies
> Her own angelic glory seems begun.[7]

---

3. Composed respectively in 1798, 1800, 1802, 1804 according to Wordsworth but more probably 1801 according to De Selincourt—see *PW, 2,* 47, 473—and 1807.

4. Stanza VIII.

5. See *The White Doe,* ll. 226–34.

6. *The Force of Prayer,* ll. 63–4, 65–8.

7. Ll. 40–2. *Maternal Grief,* written in 1812–13 after the deaths of Catherine and Thomas Wordsworth, should perhaps also be considered part of this pattern. Here again religious consolation helps; the mother finds "Dear consolation, kneeling on the turf / In prayer" (ll. 71–2).

The one poem dealing with a suffering woman that does not fit the
pattern is *Laodamia*.[8] In answer to her prayers the gods restore to
Laodamia the spirit of her husband Protesilaus, who counsels her to accept his death and

> "Learn, by a mortal yearning, to ascend—
> Seeking a higher object. Love was given,
> Encouraged, sanctioned, chiefly for that end;
> For this the passion to excess was driven—
> That self might be annulled: her bondage prove
> The fetters of a dream opposed to love."—[9]

The unfortunate Laodamia does not profit from the lesson but dies of
rebellious grief at Protesilaus' departure. In 1815 and 1820 she is not
harshly judged but is said to be delivered "from the galling yoke of
time . . . to gather flowers / Of blissful quiet." [1] By 1827, however;
her rebellion is regarded as criminal and her departed spirit is left to
wander "Apart from happy Ghosts." [2] In 1832 her punishment is re-
duced to a term in purgatory, and there Laodamia is left to "wear out
her appointed time." [3] It is noteworthy that among all the sufferers
Laodamia is the one rebel. Others either break under suffering in various
ways—they sink into apathy, they go mad, they die of grief—or they
find consolation in religion. Even including the insane, they are meek,
unrebellious sufferers, whose troubles lie beyond participation and beyond relief.

Much of the human predicament is summed up in these women, deserted, suffering, alone. It is customary to connect the theme of desertion
in Wordsworth with his treatment of Annette Vallon. It seems worth
observing that the sense of having been deserted was part of Wordsworth's own experience: he uses the word "desertion" to describe his
own feelings after the huge cliff seemed to stride after him—

> o'er my thoughts
> There hung a darkness, call it solitude,
> Or blank desertion

8. The only other possible exception is the rebellious woman of *The Excursion* who
lived torn by the two passions of avarice and maternal love. Only on her deathbed
> She, who had rebelled,
> Was into meekness softened and subdued;
> Did, after trials not in vain prolonged,
> With resignation sink into the grave.
>   VI, 771–4
It is difficult to include figures from the Pastor's tales in *The Excursion* with the figures
Wordsworth created in the *Lyrical Ballads*. The people from *The Excursion* fail to
come alive; their stories remain flat, one-dimensional illustrations.

9. Ll. 145–50.

1. *PW*, 2, *apparatus criticus*, 271–2.

2. L. 162, and *PW*, 2, *apparatus criticus*, 272.

3. L. 161.

and again when he suffered endless nightmares in consequence of the atrocities accompanying the French Revolution—

> a sense,
> Death-like, of treacherous desertion, felt
> In the last place of refuge—my own soul.[4]

The figure of the suffering woman belongs to this darkness, this death-like sense of desertion in the soul.

Wordsworth's other major figure, the old man, likewise embodies the human predicament. He first appears in the *juvenilia*, No. xv, *Fragment of a "Gothic" Tale*, presumably written about 1791.[5] Blind and helpless, the old man clearly prefigures the Baron Herbert of *The Borderers*, for both are old men led to a dungeon by a youth who plans a murder that is prevented by what seem to be supernatural signs. The Baron Herbert, in addition to being blind, is in exile from his rightful estate. He appears as a pilgrim, carrying staff and scrip, led by his daughter Idonea. Herbert's figure in many ways sums up the helplessness of man. Blind, aged, palsied, dependent on the kindness of others, Herbert is deserted not once but twice. After Marmaduke has left him to the ordeal of the bleak waste, the peasant Eldred encounters him in time to save his life but is frightened by the sight of blood and abandons the old man. Marmaduke in his remorse describes Herbert:

> And such a Man—so meek and unoffending—
> Helpless and harmless as a babe: a Man
> By obvious signal to the world's protection
> Solemnly dedicated.[6]

The helplessness of man appears even more clearly in the figure of the blind beggar of *The Prelude*. Once in a London crowd Wordsworth watched the faces of the passers-by with a sense of the mystery of other lives, oppressed

> By thoughts of what and whither, when and how,
> Until the shapes before my eyes became
> A second-sight procession, such as glides
> Over still mountains, or appears in dreams.

Far traveled in this mood, suddenly he saw the blind beggar,

> who, with upright face,
> Stood, propped against a wall, upon his chest
> Wearing a written paper, to explain
> His story, whence he came, and who he was.

4. *The Prelude*, I, 393–5; x, 413–15.
5. See *PW*, *I*, 370.
6. v, 2163–6.

Caught by the spectacle, Wordsworth's mind

> turned round
> As with the might of waters; an apt type
> This label seemed of the utmost we can know,
> Both of ourselves and of the universe;

and he stood and gazed "As if admonished from another world." [7]

Herbert's figure also connects with the ghostly soldier of *The Prelude* who seems the embodiment of solitude. The tall thin spectre of *The Vale of Esthwaite* is the first of the ghostly figures who emerge as if from another world.[8] The Beggar describes Herbert as "Lank as a ghost and tall, his shoulders bent"; [9] the soldier who looms up in the moonlight

> was of stature tall,
> A span above man's common measure, tall,
> Stiff, lank, and upright; a more meagre man
> Was never seen before by night or day.

Unlike Herbert the soldier is alone, with neither dog nor staff; the desolation and simplicity of his very dress "seem'd akin to solitude." The staff, however, is lying unseen in the grass; almost no Wordsworthian traveler appears without one.[1]

Something of the uncanniness of these old men, the sense of an apparition from another world, appears too in the old man of *Resolution and Independence*. There the leech gatherer appears as if "by peculiar grace, / A leading from above, a something given." To the despondent poet he seems "The oldest man . . . that ever wore grey hairs," a figure who in his extreme old age embodies not man's helplessness but man's power to endure. The age and impassivity of this old man make him an earth figure: he appears like a huge stone that is itself like a sea beast, "not all alive nor dead." Propped on his long gray staff, motionless, his body is bent double as if he had carried a more than human weight.[2] When the leech gatherer answers the poet's question about his employment, the poet's trancelike feeling grows stronger so that the old man's voice fades off into a stream of words and his whole body seems a dream image "Or like a man from some far region sent." [3] A lonely and

---

7. vii, 631–4, 639–42, 644–6, 649. See also for an image of man's helplessness *The Old Cumberland Beggar*.

8. *PW, 1*, 277–8, ll. 325–49.

9. *The Borderers,* i, 461.

1. *The Prelude,* iv, 391–4; iv, A, 419; iv, 427–30. James, in *The Romantic Comedy,* p. 85, compares this figure to Keats' Moneta, finding that both combine "extreme helplessness and submission to suffering and also a plenitude of power."

2. Stanzas viii–xi.

3. L. iii.

silent wanderer about the weary moors, the pilgrim figure of this old
man is at once desolate and grand, subhuman in inanimacy, superhuman
in rocklike power to endure.

The old man, of the brief poem *Animal Tranquillity and Decay* also
seems an earth figure; in his "settled quiet" and perfect peace this human animal seems to be making a gradual return to the earth from
which he came. Mortality is less happily viewed in *The Small Celandine*
and in *The Fountain,* in which the poet and Matthew both regret the
losses that age brings. Matthew lacks the supernatural qualities of soldier
and leech gatherer; he is a completely human figure. The gaiety of his
old age rises above the sadness of mortality: his dead daughter cannot
be replaced by another child; his dead children cannot be replaced by
the young poet.[4] Matthew, Simon Lee, and Timothy of *The Childless
Father* are human figures—they have a quiet acceptance of decay and
loss without the sublimity of some of Wordsworth's other old men.

The essential solitude of Wordsworth's people appears in almost all
these figures, the child alone excepted. They relate to nature—to the
earth—but seldom to other human beings. The Female Vagrant has
no earthly friend; [5] Margaret, calling for the return of her son, has "no
other earthly friend." [6] Emily Norton's sole companion is the white doe,
a somewhat unearthly friend. Michael sitting by his stone pile, Leonard
returning to sea, the leech gatherer wandering silent and alone about
the moors—all are companionless figures. Lucy Gray and the spectral
soldier of *The Prelude* are virtual embodiments of solitude. The Highland reaper sings a solitary song; the old Cumberland beggar "travels
on, a solitary Man; / His age has no companion." [7] Herbert is originally
accompanied by his daughter but is abandoned alone on the bleak waste.
Marmaduke condemns himself to be a wanderer in search of expiation,
an outcast from human society.[8] The vision is of the isolation of the
human spirit, a lonely wanderer on life's journey.

Wordsworth *saw* the human being as a solitary figure, suffering and
helpless. Since his whole major work, left unfinished at his death, was
to be called *The Recluse,* one suspects that he so saw himself. Yet his
deliberate philosophy condemned solitude as wrong and unhealthy.
The solitary human being who withdraws, rejecting contact with others,
Wordsworth condemns, both in *Lines Left upon a Seat in a Yew
Tree . . .* and in the figure of the Solitary in *The Excursion*. The con-
tradiction seems real and unresolved. Solitude Wordsworth recognized
as the condition of human life; solitude he embraced as necessary for
his work; solitude he condemned as wrong. The famous

4. *The Two April Mornings, The Fountain.*
5. *Guilt and Sorrow,* l. 446.
6. *The Affliction of Margaret* ——, l. 77.
7. *The Old Cumberland Beggar,* ll. 24, 44–5.
8. *The Borderers,* v, 2314–15.

Farewell, farewell the heart that lives alone,
Housed in a dream, at distance from the Kind!
Such happiness, wherever it be known,
Is to be pitied; for 'tis surely blind [9]

one would expect to precede the great poems about people. It does not;
almost all Wordsworth's memorable human figures were created before
1805. The volume of 1807 includes *Song at the Feast of Brougham Castle; The White Doe of Rylstone* and *The Force of Prayer* appeared in
1815. All portray persons who have "The wisdom which adversity had
bred," [1] but there are no more Margarets or Michaels. Love of Nature
may lead to love of man in *The Prelude* [2] but *The Prelude* remains a
poem of solitary moments. The creative core of man is proclaimed solitary:

Imagination having been our theme,
So also hath that intellectual Love,
For they are each in each, and cannot stand
Dividually.—Here must thou be, O Man!
Power to thyself; no Helper hast thou here;
Here keepest thou in singleness thy state:
No other can divide with thee this work:
No secondary hand can intervene
To fashion this ability; 'tis thine,
The prime and vital principle is thine
In the recesses of thy nature, far
From any reach of outward fellowship,
Else is not thine at all.[3]

Like the solitary the wanderer is a recurrent figure, subsuming Wordsworth's other figures, central to his vision of human life. Some of the
fascination that the wandering figure held for Wordsworth may be explained by his account of his love of roads:

I love a public road: few sights there are
That please me more; such object hath had power
O'er my imagination since the dawn
Of childhood, when its disappearing line,
Seen daily afar off, on one bare steep
Beyond the limits which my feet had trod
Was like a guide into eternity,
At least to things unknown and without bound.
Even something of the grandeur which invests

9. *Elegiac Stanzas Suggested by a Picture of Peele Castle,* ll. 53–6.
1. *Song at the Feast of Brougham Castle,* l. 168.
2. Bk. VIII.
3. XIV, 206–18.

The Mariner who sails the roaring sea
Through storm and darkness early in my mind
Surrounded, too, the Wanderers of the Earth,
Grandeur as much, and loveliness far more.[4]

The dignity of the sailor's mother and the beggar woman seems to derive in part from their being journeyers; much of the strangeness of
the leech gatherer comes from the image of his lonely and silent wandering. Life is seen as a journey with eternity its bound: we all step
westward. Exiles from our native home—see Herbert, the Female
Vagrant, Leonard, and the *Intimations* ode—we wander in search of
the paradise that we have lost. Herbert is a pilgrim figure, carrying
staff and scrip; the ghostly soldier, the old Cumberland beggar, the
leech gatherer have their pilgrim staffs. Emily Norton wanders "long
and far" before she returns to Rylstone, wearing woolen garb that suits
"A wandering Pilgrim's humbleness." [5]

The Wanderer of *The Excursion* epitomizes this aspect of human
existence. But just as the Solitary in that poem is only a partial embodiment, presenting the negative aspects of solitude with none of its positive aspects, so the Wanderer of *The Excursion* is a partial figure. The
other wanderers are all suffering figures; only the Wanderer is not.
"He had no painful pressure from without" but "could *afford* to suffer / With those whom he saw suffer." [6] Since the Wanderer lacks a
core of suffering, he ceases to share the human problem; he has never
been exiled from Paradise and has no real cause to be a wanderer.

A curious disparity exists, moreover, between the advice the Wanderer gives to the Solitary and Wordsworth's picture of the Wanderer
himself. The Wanderer counsels the Solitary that his disillusionment in
consequence of the outcome of the French Revolution is unreasonable;
he was disillusioned only because he had expected too much of humanity.[7] The implication of the stories that the Pastor tells is that knowledge of human beings as they are is sufficient: some conquer their anguish, some abuse their talents, but whether theirs is a spiritual triumph
or failure, the stories tend, according to the Wanderer,

"to patience when affliction strikes;
To hope and love; to confident repose
In God; and reverence for the dust of Man." [8]

The character of the Wanderer himself, however, seems an image of
idealized perfection; Wordsworth draws in him a figure of love and wis-

4. XII, A, 145–57.
5. *The White Doe,* ll. 1610–11.
6. I, 368; see Notes, *PW*, 5, 387, "He had no painful pressure from within." *The Excursion,* I, 370–1.
7. IV, 260 ff.
8. VII, 1055–7.

dom unblemished by human failing. Having grown up among the mountains, having known the sense "Of visitation from the living God," the Wanderer has a "Sublime and comprehensive" being, with no low thoughts or desires but meekness of heart and wisdom of mind.[9] The advice is to accept human imperfection; the image is of perfection. Since the Wanderer's solution for the problem of human suffering is not rooted in personal conquest of suffering or mastery of human fraility, one is tempted to think that the solution depends on the absence of the problem.

Set against Wordsworth's other old men, both the Wanderer and the Solitary of *The Excursion* lack something. The Wanderer, although idealized, is most satisfactory in the passages of Book 1 in which he is described as a solitary figure, watching the hills grow larger in the darkness, watching the world at sunrise lie before him in gladness.[1] The solitary wanderer seems to be Wordsworth's central image for the human being: when the Solitary does not wander and the Wanderer ceases to be solitary, the vision seems to be disintegrating.

Taken collectively, the Wordsworth human—child, young girl, joyous irresponsible, suffering woman, and enduring old man—emerges as a figure with distinct limitations. The child, the young girl, the joyous irresponsible all have an inner life and activity that one misses in the suffering woman who withdraws from life under her burden of sorrow and in the old man who passively endures. There is no real figure of active conquest of suffering. Clearly Wordsworth, in the good Lord Clifford, in Emily Norton, in young Romilly's mother, intended to portray this conquest. The good Lord Clifford rejects "Revenge, and all ferocious thoughts," but the only description we are given of constructive action is

> Love had he found in huts where poor men lie;
> His daily teachers had been woods and rills,
> The silence that is in the starry sky,
> The sleep that is among the lonely hills.[2]

The lines are beautiful, but the progression from *love* to *silence* and *sleep* does not represent constructive action. *The White Doe* conveys, as Harper observed, "a sense of the futility and transitoriness of action." [3] While several of the figures of *The Excursion*—the disappointed lover, betrayed Ellen, the good clergyman, etc.—achieve a conquest over unhappiness, their very deadness makes their stories seem little more than exempla. *The Happy Warrior,* a title that implies the ac-

9. See 1, 212, 219–43.
1. 1, 125–31, 197–218.
2. *Song at the Feast of Brougham Castle,* ll. 166, 161–4.
3. George M. Harper, *William Wordsworth: His Life, Works, and Influence* (New York, Scribners, 1916), 2, 155.

tivity one misses in the adult figures, offers not a concrete person but
an abstract ideal.

Moreover, the human being merges into the landscape—into rocks
and stones and trees—until the human is almost as inert and motionless
as the vegetable creation. The result of the tendency to see persons as
natural and nature as human is to dehumanize the human being. At
Wordsworth's best, of course, human and natural are both spiritual,
but frequently, as in *Nutting* and *Hart-Leap Well,* nature is spiritual and
man is deforming. In Wordsworth's vision mankind darkens creation:
in the "Prospectus" of *The Excursion* he turns reluctantly from his
theme of the glory of the inner world of mind to the outer world of men:

> —Such grateful haunts foregoing, if I oft
> Must turn elsewhere—to travel near the tribes
> And fellowships of men, and see ill sights
> Of madding passions mutually inflamed;
> Must hear Humanity in fields and groves
> Pipe solitary anguish; or must hang
> Brooding above the fierce confederate storm
> Of sorrow [4]

He asks that he may record this vision too.

Wordsworth fulfilled this ambition in the *Lyrical Ballads* and in the
Poems of 1807. Outside this period he seems to have been unable to
project vital power into the human figure. The early *An Evening Walk*
and *Descriptive Sketches* are scenic poems in which persons amount to
little more than additional scenic effects—sometimes scenic blots. "Here,
where no trace of man the spot profanes" [5] seems to indicate a preference for nature without man. And in the late poetry the human being
has virtually vanished.[6]

Regardless of these limitations, the Wordsworth human being, like
the Wordsworth landscape, is the vehicle of an impressive vision. The
essential vision is of the plight of man—his loneliness, his helplessness,
his suffering. Herbert journeys blind and helpless into betrayal; Michael
sits by his stone pile; the leech gatherer wanders silent and alone across
the weary moors; Margaret questions the unanswering darkness of
dungeon or desert or deep for her son. The conscious philosophy attempted an answer to the problem of human suffering, but there is no
corresponding vision, except perhaps in *Peter Bell.* The attempt at such

---

4. Ll. 72–9.
5. *Descriptive Sketches,* 1793, l. 425.
6. See *Memorials of a Tour on the Continent, 1820,* and *Memorials of a Tour in Italy,
1837,* all of which are poems about places. *Fish-Women.—On Landing at Calais* again
treats persons as scenic effects. If *The Armenian Lady's Love* (1830), *The Russian Fugi-
tive* (1828), and *The Egyptian Maid* (1828) can be termed poems about persons, the
persons are remarkable for their unreality.

a vision in the person of the Wanderer was doomed to failure, since the Wanderer had no inner darkness.

It is not easy to say why, when Wordsworth's suffering women and enduring old men speak so clearly of the anguish of life and the helplessness of humanity, the final effect is one of tranquillity. In *Michael* and *The Ruined Cottage* the suffering is diminished in intensity by aesthetic distancing: Michael is dead and only the ruined stone pile remains; Margaret is gone and the weeds and spear grass silvered over with mist stand tranquil. Yet the monologues of the women lack this distancing: the forsaken Indian woman and the mad mother and the Margaret who seeks news of her missing son speak from the living heart of their trouble. The fact that Wordsworth's suffering people lack rebellion, that they accept their suffering, is perhaps a partial explanation. A more adequate explanation may be the fact that these poems endorse the human heart. The dignity of these simple people lies in their capacity for feeling; in their lonely suffering they embody at once the human predicament and the human achievement.

The essential vision includes, too, something beyond both human predicament and human achievement. The figures that matter most are the solitary wanderers, coming from and journeying into infinity and keeping about them on their earthly journey something of the strangeness of that other world. Landscape and human being alike convey the unknown modes of being.

V

Sounds, Waters, and Man-made Structures

AS one turns from the people in the landscape to Wordsworth's other major symbols—sounds, waters, and man-made structures —symbol, metaphor, and simile cross and recross. Wordsworthian landscape and Wordsworthian human have concerned us primarily on the level of symbol. Landscape and people interlock with the great cross current of metaphor and simile in which the natural is alive and the human is natural, but there are few metaphors or similes that present miniature landscapes or persons. Water and architectural structures appear both as symbols and as metaphor and simile: water in *The River Duddon* is symbol and in the *Ecclesiastical Sonnets* metaphor; the religious structure of Book v of *The Excursion* is literal and perhaps symbolic whereas the temple which the Wanderer praises in Book III, ll. 32 ff. and 115 ff., is metaphoric.

The voices that sound in the landscape exist like the landscape itself primarily as symbols. Since sounds are properties of things, it may be objected that they should not be made parallel to water and to buildings, which are things. I have been able to discover no way out of this difficulty: sounds in the Wordsworthian landscape do have symbolic value and must be regarded as themselves things. Sounds and silence were clearly poles of attraction for Wordsworth: sounds speak of life, its terror, joy, anguish, and mystery; silence speaks of the unknown and of peace. As sounds fade away into silence, both symbolize the mysterious and invisible.

The human sounds in the Wordsworthian landscape are most often sad. As one might expect, the still, sad music of humanity is largely unheard in the *juvenilia*: Orpheus sings "his tale of sorrow o'er and o'er" [1] and the cottage woman sings a "plaintive-sad" lullaby to her child, [2] but otherwise the sounds are not those of humanity. Human sounds in *An Evening Walk* are distant and faintly heard; [3] they are clearer in *Descriptive Sketches* [4] but are still for the most part lost among the sounds of nature. The voice of the Female Vagrant in *Guilt and Sor-*

1. *Orpheus and Eurydice, PW, 1,* 284, l. 48.
2. Juvenilia XVI, *PW, 1,* 294, ll. 70–4.
3. See ll. 143–5, 321, 438.
4. See ll. 53–79, where the voice of blasphemy breaks into the silence of Chartreuse, and ll. 594–621, where the swain protests against the poverty that forces members of a family to separate.

row first sounds the music of humanity in all its sadness. The monologues of Wordsworth's suffering women—the soliloquy of the mad mother, the complaint of the forsaken Indian woman, the lament of the emigrant mother, the despairing question of Margaret—voice solitary anguish. The solitary reaper's song is at once melancholy and mysterious; the poet does not know its subject and it is the more melancholy for its unknown burden. There are few comparable masculine voices. The embittered talk of Oswald and the Solitary is in each case part of a larger pattern: their melodies are not meant to be final. Marmaduke's self-rejection ends *The Borderers* on a note of despair; the solitary soldier who

> Sent forth a murmuring voice of dead complaint,
> Groans scarcely audible [5]

is the true voice of desolation. He, however, like the old leech gatherer, is also the voice of one from some far region sent. Soldier and leech gatherer have about them something of the mystery that is in the solitary reaper's song.

A human voice of joy (except for Wordsworth's own) is rare. Dorothy's voice "was like a hidden Bird that sang"; [6] in Wordsworth's worst crisis, "like a brook / That did but *cross* a lonely road," [7] she was able to restore him to himself. During the early days of the French Revolution "A homeless sound of joy was in the sky" but nothing remained of it later except a hollow " 'Good morrow, Citizen!' " [8] The idiot boy's joyous burring and the mirth of the idle shepherd boys are, except for the soothing voices of Wanderer and Pastor in *The Excursion,* the only completely happy human voices that one hears.

One senses a certain distaste for normal human noise. Not only does Wordsworth dislike personal talk and neighborly gossip,[9] he dislikes crowded city streets and noise and confusion. St. Bartholomew's Fair he describes as "a hell / For eyes and ears," "Monstrous in colour, motion, shape, sight, sound." The city with its swarm of inhabitants is just "blank confusion"; Wordsworth is grateful for "release / From social noise." [1] Since the human sound is so seldom joyful, since what the poet hears is "solitary anguish" or "the fierce confederate storm / Of sorrow," [2] it is not surprising that the proportion of human sound in the landscape is small.

Nor did man-made music greatly interest Wordsworth. Notes of

5. *The Prelude,* IV, A, 431–2.
6. *The Recluse,* l. 91.
7. *The Prelude,* XI, 337–8.
8. *Composed near Calais, on the Road Leading to Ardres, August 7, 1802,* ll. 5, 11.
9. *Personal Talk.*
1. *The Prelude,* VII, A, 658–9; VII, 688, 722. *At Dover,* ll. 6–7.
2. *Prospectus to The Excursion,* ll. 77–9.

music floating across the air are part of the stray pleasures of this earth;[3] the real power of music is its power to lift human beings out of reality and give them momentary happiness.[4] The music that did stir Wordsworth was the natural song of life that rose from all living things:

> beast and bird, the lamb,
> The shepherd's dog, the linnet and the thrush,
> Vied with this waterfall, and made a song
> Which, while I listened, seemed like the wild growth
> Or like some natural produce of the air,
> That could not cease to be.[5]

The "thousand blended notes" of the song of life sound to the fleshly ear, but the song was

> Most audible, then, when the fleshly ear,
> O'ercome by humblest prelude of that strain,
> Forgot her functions, and slept undisturbed.

The "blessed power that rolls / About, below, above" seems itself to be harmony; the man who hears it can frame the measure of his soul from it and tune his being to love.[6]

The emotional expressiveness of bird song Wordsworth records with loving fidelity. The owl's hoot is sometimes terrifying;[7] sometimes the noise of owls is a "concourse wild / Of jocund din";[8] sometimes their cry is almost humorous.

> The owlets through the long blue night
> Are shouting to each other still:
> Fond lovers! yet not quite hob nob,
> They lengthen out the tremulous sob,
> That echoes far from hill to hill.[9]

The lark's is a more constant sound, its song a note of joy contrasting with human "Labour and grief and Solitude and fear."[1] The nightingale mourns[2] or pours out a song of fiery passion, and the poet prefers the stock dove's pensive song of love and serious faith.[3a] The thrush's

---

3. *Stray Pleasures.*
4. *Power of Music;* see also "The fairest, brightest, hues of ether fade."
5. "It was an April morning: fresh and clear," ll. 25–30.
6. *Lines Written in Early Spring,* l. 1; *The Prelude,* II, 416–18; *To My Sister,* ll. 33–6.
7. *The Vale of Esthwaite, PW, I,* 271, ll. 51–2; 274, ll. 200–8.
8. "There was a Boy," ll. 15–16.
9. *The Idiot Boy,* ll. 287–91. See also the sympathetic account in "The leaves that rustled on this oak-crowned hill." Is the "lone bell-bird" tolling from its perch also the owl? *On the Power of Sound,* l. 27.
1. *In Part from Moschus—Lament for Bion, PW, I,* 287, ll. 16–21. See also the two poems *To a Skylark.*
2. *Orpheus and Eurydice, PW, I,* 284, ll. 51–8.
3a. "O Nightingale! thou surely art."

note is one of enchantment: it summons up for poor Susan a vision of home; it summons the poet out into the wind and rain to sing along with it. Its song provides a symbol of the poet's own.[4]

But the cuckoo is pre-eminently Wordsworth's bird. It is a "wandering Voice," invisible, mysterious, its sovereign cry invariably associated with the coming of spring, with sunshine and flowers.[5] The thrilling voice whose bodily source remains unseen calls up for the poet an equally unsubstantial world, the golden time of youth when the poet was full of hope.[6] Years later the cuckoo had still its prophetic power, "Wandering in solitude, and evermore / Foretelling and proclaiming," but the proclamation had become less of visionary hours than of the advent of our Lord.[7]

Bird song and the sound of the wind alike fascinated Wordsworth because of their freedom from human limitation and because of the invisibility of the source of the sound.

> Admonishing the man who walks below
> Of solitude, and silence in the sky

the bird is a "pilgrim of the sky" and almost by spatial contiguity leads into thoughts of eternity. The Wanderer reminds the Solitary of the sound of the raven fading in the distance at dusk "with echoes from afar / Faint—and still fainter." [8]

The sound of the wind, always invisible in source, leads even more directly to the "visionary power." The wind is "The ghostly language of the ancient earth," a "strange utterance" that makes the sky seem "not a sky / Of earth" and the motion of the clouds mysterious. The power of sound can "breathe an elevated mood, by form / Or image unprofaned"; from such moods of "shadowy exultation" Wordsworth "retains an obscure sense / Of possible sublimity." [9]

Echoes too touch the ear with "visionary impulses" and lead to thoughts of another world.[1] The power of sound to suggest the invisible is nowhere expressed more clearly than in the late *On the Power of Sound*. There Wordsworth links the power of music with reason, finding in the harmonies of music earthly evidence of a divine art. The song of life had come to be dominated by the thud of earth dropping on the

4. *The Reverie of Poor Susan*, "Hark! 'tis the Thrush, undaunted, undeprest," and *Prelude Prefixed to the Volume Entitled "Poems Chiefly of Early and Late Years,"* ll. 1–14, 33–42.
5. "The sun has long been set"; *To the Cuckoo,* two poems; *The Solitary Reaper; The Cuckoo at Laverna;* and *The Cuckoo-Clock.*
6. *To the Cuckoo* (O blithe New-comer!).
7. *The Cuckoo at Laverna,* ll. 98–9.
8. *The Recluse,* ll. 132–3; *To a Skylark* (Ethereal minstrel!), l. 1; *The Excursion,* IV, 1178 ff.
9. *The Prelude,* I, 330–9; II, 302–22. See also I, 35; V, 595–7.
1. See *To Joanna,* "Yes, it was the mountain Echo," and *Echo upon the Gemmi.*

coffin, by the convict's summons, by the distress gun; [2] the poet now sought a scale of "moral music" telling "Of the Unsubstantial." Believing that

> By one pervading spirit
> Of tones and numbers all things are controlled,

he still heard all sounds as part of a universal harmony;

> All worlds, all natures, mood and measure keep
> For praise and ceaseless gratulation, poured
> Into the ear of God, their Lord! [3]

Even more than sound, silence could seem the symbol of the spiritual. Distant sounds from an invisible source lead the mind to thoughts of infinity; silence is the best language of the spirit. The voiceless glowworm shining beneath the ferns summoned Wordsworth to continue *The Prelude* just as the music of the redbreasts had;

> Silence touched me here
> No less than sound had done before. [4]

The language of the twin peaks that speak to the Solitary, in addition to the sounds of wind and water, includes

> Music of finer tone; a harmony,
> So do I call it, though it be the hand
> Of silence, though there be no voice;—the clouds,
> The mist, the shadows, light of golden suns,
> Motion of moonlight, all come thither—touch,
> And have an answer—thither come, and shape
> A language not unwelcome to sick hearts. [5]

The Wanderer, hearkening to the lamb's cry, "The plaintive spirit of the solitude!" is silent

> Through consciousness that silence in such place
> Was best, the most affecting eloquence. [6]

The "silence and the calm / Of mute insensate things" [7] was part of the healing power of nature and could lead the listener back to life.

Yet silence, like solitude, is not altogether to be praised. The silence that surrounds Hart-Leap Well is doleful and morbid, part of the absence of life that is Nature's curse upon the place. Even the silence that

---

2. Stanzas VII, X.
3. Ll. 170, 176, 177–8, 206–8.
4. VII, 36–7.
5. *The Excursion*, II, 710–16.
6. IV, 412, 414–15.
7. "Three years she grew in sun and shower," ll. 17–18.

Wordsworth desires in *Personal Talk* is "barren." [8] It is after all the tomb that is silent.[9] The natural affinities of silence are "ghostly Shapes" that meet at noontide;

> Fear and trembling Hope,
> Silence and Foresight; Death the Skeleton
> And Time the Shadow.[1]

Perhaps for this reason Wordsworth in *On the Power of Sound* refuses to equate the "central peace" with "eternal Silence." In lines that recall the *Intimations* ode he asks

> O Silence! are man's noisy years
> No more than moments of thy life?

and answers

> No! though earth be dust
> And vanish, though the heavens dissolve, her stay
> Is in the WORD, that shall not pass away.[2]

The "dread Voice that speaks from out the sea / Of God's eternal Word" [3] is of course no natural sound. Silence and sound alike lead to something other than themselves.

The alert reader must be aware that my discussion of sound has omitted what is perhaps the most characteristic Wordsworthian sound of all—the sound of water. Water in all its aspects—its sound and its quiet, its movement and its peace, its transparency and its power to reflect—is one of Wordsworth's most all-pervasive vehicles. It is also one of his most troublesome to discuss because the literal stream often seems to exist for its own sake with little if any symbolic value and because the metaphorical uses of water are all inclusive. Some of the difficulties will become clear simply from consideration of Wordsworth's first [4] "water" poem—the *Lines Written near Richmond, upon the*

---

8. 1, 10.

9. See "Surprised by joy—impatient as the wind," l. 3; *The River Duddon*, XXIV, l. 12; and the lines printed as *The Death of a Starling—Catullus*, ll. 12–16, *PW*, 1, 263:

> Thou, in peace, in silence sleeping
> In some still world, unknown, remote
> The mighty Parent's care hast found,
> Without whose tender guardian thought
> No Sparrow falleth to the ground.

Smyser, "Coleridge's Use of Wordsworth's Juvenilia," *PMLA*, 65 (June, 1950), 423–6, argues convincingly that these lines are a separate poem and not part of *The Death of a Starling—Catullus*.

1. *Yew-Trees*, ll. 25–8.

2. Ll. 217–18, 222–4.

3. *At Dover*, 11–12.

4. There is no single poem in the *juvenilia* that deals with brook or lake or ocean; but the two descriptions of moonlight on Winander (*Beauty and Moonlight*, ll. 5–6, and *The Dog—An Idyllium*, ll. 4–6), the account of the experience of the "mystic dream" beside Esthwaite (*The Vale of Esthwaite*, l. 76), the observation of the reflection in

Thames, at Evening.[5] Here Wordsworth draws an analogy between the darkness of the stream behind the boat as evening settles and the gloom that may well overtake the hopes of the youthful poet. The poet then wishes that the quiet movement of the water may lead the mind to flow in equal quiet; dismissing this wish, he finds in the brightness, solemnity, and serenity of the water "The image of a poet's heart." The river in this poem suggests successive ideas to the poet but is never a fully realized symbol.[6]

The two most fully realized water symbols appear in *The Prelude* and in *The River Duddon.* Kenneth MacLean in his article "The Water Symbol in *The Prelude* (1805–06)" [7] has already dealt with water throughout *The Prelude.* MacLean first quotes extensively the literal water passages, making no distinction between literal and symbolic, and then discusses the water metaphors. In his terms water exists as symbol in *The Prelude* in the sense of recurrent and central metaphor. Water, he finds, provides images for the mind and its powers, for the imagination, and for poetry. His discussion makes plain that the water metaphors gain in significance and weight from the presence of so much actual water; 1 should add that the recurrent water metaphors in turn lend weight to the water symbol of the great climactic scene on Mount Snowdon. Literal and metaphoric waters seem to me to be held together by this scene of the poet on the mountain, looking over the

---

Grasmere of "The lone grey cots and pastoral steeps" (*Septimi Gades,* ll. 22–4), and the description of the ocean shuddering at the sound of the sunset cannon (*At the Isle of Wight*) all point to the poet's interest in water. See *PW*, I, 263, 264, 271, 297, 307–8.

5. Divided from 1800 on, with stanzas 1 and 2 printed as *Lines Written While Sailing in a Boat at Evening* and the remainder in 1802 given the title *Remembrance of Collins.*

6. The poem seems to be an early, unsuccessful attempt, partially literal description, partially discovering a tenor in a vehicle. Wordsworth's thought moves between the actual stream and the mind; as the poem progresses, he comes closer and closer to seeing the mind in the water scene. In the analogy (Such views the youthful Bard allure) the poet's hopes are the center of interest; the water lingers as vehicle. When next Wordsworth turns to the mind,

    O glide! fair stream! for ever so,
    Thy quiet soul on all bestowing,
    Till all our minds for ever flow
    As thy deep waters now are flowing,

there is attraction between the river and the mind—the mind is to flow—but the mind is not yet altogether seen in the water. Finally, in

    Vain thought!—Yet be as now thou art
    That in thy waters may be seen
    The image of a poet's heart,
    How bright, how solemn, how serene!

the mind and the water are momentarily one. In a fully realized symbol the literal object remains the center of attention; it is river and something more. The something more may become very explicit—in Wordsworth it usually does—but it is discovered in, not added to, the literal object. Here Wordsworth at once drops the something more and the rest of the poem is merely descriptive.

7. *University of Toronto Quarterly,* 17 (July, 1948), 372–89.

moonlit sea of mist covering the surrounding hills and hearing from a distant chasm the roar of waters.

> The universal spectacle throughout
> Was shaped for admiration and delight,
> Grand in itself alone, but in that breach
> Through which the homeless voice of waters rose,
> That dark deep thoroughfare had Nature lodg'd
> The Soul, the Imagination of the Whole.[8]

The voice that issues from the dark abyss is here virtually the voice of God: the scene itself is the "image of a mighty Mind" and the voices that issue forth "to silent light" are in the early version the divine under-presence in one's own soul and in the later version "recognitions of transcendent power." [9] The dark depths of the mind, like the "deep and gloomy breathing-place through which / Mounted the roar of waters," send up the voice of waters: the faculty of intellectual love, imagination, or "reason in her most exalted mood" is a stream that springs from darkness and leads to "the great thought / By which we live, Infinity and God." The recurrent water metaphors for the movement of the poem as a whole, for the life stream of a human being, and for the stream of consciousness in the mind [1] are drawn together in the water symbol of the last book of *The Prelude*. In the beginning of the poem the ceaseless music of the river Derwent symbolizes the music of poetry; [2] in the end the water symbol unites poetry and imagination and poet.

The River Duddon seems on one level almost *The Prelude* in reverse. In *The Prelude* Wordsworth writes of his own life and constantly draws on water imagery; *The River Duddon* is directly about a river and indirectly about Wordsworth himself.[3] He turns to the Duddon's story in relief, even as he had begun his explicitly biographical poem in relief from more difficult themes.

> Better to breathe at large on this clear height
> Than toil in needless sleep from dream to dream:
> Pure flow the verse, pure, vigorous, free, and bright,
> For Duddon, long-loved Duddon, is my theme![4]

8. XIII, A, 60–5.
9. XIII, A, 69, 71–3; XIV, 73–7.
1. XIII, A, 57–8, 166 ff., 183–4 quoted. VII, 1–12; IX, 1–8. XIV, 368–9. III, 139–40; VI, 742 ff.; I, 211 ff.; IV, 256 ff. I am indebted to Kenneth MacLean for most of these references.
2. I, 269 ff.
3. See also the sonnet *To the River Derwent*.
4. I, 11–14. Clearly the river here also provides the image for the flow of the poetry itself.

The Duddon's function, "to heal and to restore, / To soothe and cleanse, not madden and pollute!" sounds remarkably like Wordsworth's own ideal for himself as a poet; the river's "Bright liquid mansions" which endure when "the solidities of mortal pride" have crumbled [5] remind one of the mansion of verse that is also a transparent veil.[6]

It may be well not to insist on this particular symbolism: certainly there lies behind the image of the river's birth and growth the parallel birth and growth of human life in general. The river is a "Child of the clouds" whose foster mother is the earth; it is a "cradled Nursling" with a clear voice which grows into "a Brook of loud and stately march." [7] The steppingstones across it "might seem a zone / Chosen for ornament"; the union of the river and its tributary stream is described in terms suitable for human marriage; the river's advance to the sea suggests the mingling of the soul with eternity.[8] So strong is the suggestion of human life that the river in the sonnet sequence is called Leader and Wanderer.[9]

But while the river Duddon like man is born and grows, unlike man it does not pass away. It is therefore, as Beatty has observed, "a type of the ever-vanishing yet ever developing race of man." [1] It is also an immutability symbol. The river flows on, though the mighty forests where bison and huge deer once stalked have disappeared, though the "solidities of mortal pride, / Palace and tower, are crumbled into dust!" [2] Human life seen against the permanence of nature is transitory:

Still glides the Stream, and shall for ever glide;
The Form remains, the Function never dies;
While we, the brave, the mighty, and the wise,
We Men, who in our morn of youth defied
The elements, must vanish;—be it so! [3]

Water images abound, of course, outside *The Prelude* and *The River Duddon,* though elsewhere they are less central and occur usually not as symbol but as metaphor. MacLean's grouping for *The Prelude*—of water as vehicle for the mind and its powers, for the imagination, and for poetry—omits what are throughout the main body of Wordsworth's poetry some most important uses of water.[4] Water appears as a vehicle

---

5. VIII, 13–14; XII, 7–9.
6. *The Prelude,* v, 595–605.
7. *The River Duddon,* II, 1; III, 14; IV, 1; V, 2; IX, 2.
8. IX, 4–5; XIX; XXXIII.
9. XXVIII, 14; XXXIII, 7.
1. Beatty, *William Wordsworth: His Doctrine and Art in Their Historical Relations,* p. 222.
2. II, 9–14; XII, 9–10.
3. XXXIV, 5–9. The fact that Wordsworth is here translating Horace *Epistulae* i.2.43, "At ille / Labitur, et labetur in omne volubilis aevum," supports the sense of the stream that abides though the individual perishes.
4. It would be possible of course to supplement MacLean's discussion with images

for the current of emotion, for the streams of life and time, and for
the streams of liberty and religion.

Water is of course a natural image for emotion [5] and, since feeling
is basic to life, an equally natural image for life itself. Nature has dealt
with Wordsworth

> as with a turbulent Stream,
> Some nursling of the mountains, whom she leads
> Through quiet meadows, after he has learnt
> His strength.[6]

Young Hartley Coleridge is not the stream but a faery voyager upon a
stream so clear that it seems unearthly.[7] The sonnet "Brook! whose
society the Poet seeks" makes water a pure life symbol altogether
divorced from human nature:

> It seems the Eternal Soul is clothed in thee
> With purer robes than those of flesh and blood,
> And hath bestowed on thee a safer good;
> Unwearied joy, and life without its cares.

Wordsworth's strong sense of life in water perhaps helps to account for
the central position of water in *The Prelude*.[8]

The water metaphors for the streams of freedom and religion seem
less natural. The sound of water is the voice of the landscape; by exten-
sion the voices of mountain torrents and of the ocean are the music of
liberty.[9] British freedom is a "Flood," a "most famous Stream," though
England at times seemed to Wordsworth "a fen / Of stagnant waters." [1]
When he rebukes the men of the western world for their misgovernment
he checks himself with the injunction:

> Dive through the stormy surface of the flood
> To the great current flowing underneath;
> Explore the countless springs of silent good.[2]

---

drawn from the rest of Wordsworth's poetry. For other images associating water and
poetry see especially *A Poet's Epitaph*, ll. 39–40, and the sonnet *"A Poet! He hath put
his heart to school"*; for other images connecting water and the mind see especially *The
Recluse*, ll. 292 ff., and *The Excursion*, IX, 437 ff., 462–73.

5. See *A Complaint; The Prelude*, XI, 184–5; *The Excursion*, V, 1002–7.

6. *The Recluse*, ll. 728 ff. Cf. *The Excursion*, III, 967 ff.

7. *To H. C. Six Years Old*.

8. In *The Longest Day* time like life is a river, and the sea to which it flows is of course
eternity. The "mighty Being" of "It is a beauteous evening, calm and free" links ocean and
divine life; the sonnet "Near Anio's stream, I spied a gentle Dove" links ocean and "This
sea of life . . . the living Now."

9. See "It was an April morning: fresh and clear," *Lines Written in Expectation of
the Death of Mr. Fox*, and *Thought of a Briton on the Subjugation of Switzerland*.

1. "It is not to be thought of that the Flood" and "Milton! thou shouldst be living at
this hour."

2. "Men of the Western World! in Fate's dark book," ll. 10–12.

The *Ecclesiastical Sonnets* use water imagery for the development of the church with such frequency throughout the series that water sounds as an undercurrent even where it is not mentioned. Here the image seems completely arbitrary:

> I, who accompanied with faithful pace
> Cerulean Duddon from its cloud-fed spring,
> And loved with spirit ruled by his to sing
> Of mountain-quiet and boon nature's grace;
> I, who essayed the nobler Stream to trace
> Of Liberty, and smote the plausive string
> Till the checked torrent, proudly triumphing,
> Won for herself a lasting resting-place;
> Now seek upon the heights of Time the source
> Of a HOLY RIVER, on whose banks are found
> Sweet pastoral flowers, and laurels that have crowned
> Full oft the unworthy brow of lawless force;
> And, for delight of him who tracks its course,
> Immortal amaranth and palms abound.[3]

In the end the "living Waters" lead to "the eternal City—built / For the perfècted Spirits of the just!" [4]

Water,[5] then, is one of Wordsworth's most frequently employed vehicles, literal river being reinforced by metaphor and simile to make symbolic values more explicit. It is a constant image, dominating *The Prelude,* sounding more faintly in *The Excursion,* focal in *The River Duddon,* providing a frame of reference for the *Ecclesiastical Sonnets.* At first highly subjective in value, it becomes by the time of the *Ecclesiastical Sonnets* an image for an external, objective reality. MacLean has commented on the suitability of water as an image for the life of the mind since it suggests the substantial character of thought and the union of thought and thing thought of. Even more basically, I think, water images life and links life with feeling; to live is to feel, and while the currents of feeling flow freely in the mind the streams of poetry and life run freely too.

Like water man-made structures are a constantly employed vehicle,

3. See Pt. I, II, 14; v, 14; xxxvii, I; Pt. II, vii, 1-8; viii, 1-3; Pt. III, xii, 1-14; xxxviii, 1-9; xlvii entire.

4. Pt. I, I; Pt. III, xlvii, 11-14.

5. Wordsworth's tendency in the later poetry to develop set pieces that have no value beyond that of description should perhaps be remarked. He writes with affection of the Avon and the Eden; he records literally the noise of the river Greta and the unremitting voice of nightly streams (*To the River Greta, near Keswick,* "The unremitting voice of nightly streams"). He is attracted by the transparent purity of the sea (*By the Sea-shore, Isle of Man*); he delights in the reflections in the brook (Lyre! though such power do in thy magic live). These water descriptions, while pleasant, lack the power of reverberation that the literal as symbol possesses.

though the character of the structure alters as the character of water cannot. The earliest architectural structures appear in the *juvenilia* in the castle of the *Fragment of a "Gothic" Tale* and the hut of *Incipient Madness*.[6] Both are ruined structures. The first shows the effects of "The unimaginable touch of time"[7] and is also the scene of meditated murder; the second, which for the moment must be left for separate discussion, is the abode of a mind "denied / The common food of hope."[8] The ruin of Stonehenge in *Guilt and Sorrow* and the ruined castle and deserted chapel of *The Borderers* are further developments of the ruin heavy with the sense of the dark and barbaric past linked with present crime. Both are part of the bleak wasteland landscape. Stonehenge, "Inmate of lonesome Nature's endless year," remains as a record of the terror and violence of man's destruction of his fellow men;[9] it and the Gothic castle of the *juvenilia* are both hellish places where the demons rise.[1] Within Stonehenge "that fabric of mysterious form / Winds met in conflict,"[2] and there seems a latent suggestion of the conflict in the soul of the sailor who has recently committed murder. The dungeon of the half-ruined castle where Oswald urges Marmaduke on to the murder of Herbert relates more clearly to the mind itself. Marmaduke, hesitating to descend into the dungeon, finds that

> in plumbing the abyss for judgment,
> Something I strike upon which turns my mind
> Back on herself . . . my breast
> Concentres all the terrors of the Universe.

In the dungeon occur the hallucinations that objectify the forces of the mind protesting against the murder of Herbert.[3] Stonehenge and ruined castle both loom as records of man's capacity for barbarism, a capacity that still exists in the dark abysses of the self.

After the early poems man's violence and destructiveness recede into the background. The vanished pleasure house of *Hart-Leap Well* again links ruin and desolation with human crime, but the monstrousness of the crime has diminished. Of the great lodge that Sir Walter had built in his unfeeling triumph nothing remains—only the lifeless stumps of the trees that once formed Sir Walter's bower, only the stones that

---

6. See also the castle, the dungeon, and the Gothic mansion that appear and reappear in *The Vale of Esthwaite*, *PW*, *I*, 270 ff., ll. 39–54, 212–67, 311–38.

7. *PW*, *I*, 288, l. 66.

8. *PW*, *I*, 316, ll. 59–60.

9. *Guilt and Sorrow*, ll. 121, 122–3. Cf. *The Prelude*, XIII, 312–35, where Wordsworth links his own creative power with a vision of this darkness from the past. See also *The Excursion*, III, 143–8, and IX, 690–709.

1. *PW*, *I*, *apparatus criticus* (MS I, ll. 116–35), 100, and *Fragment of a "Gothic" Tale*, ll. 26–7, 82–6 (*PW*, *I*, 287, 289).

2. *Guilt and Sorrow*, ll. 127–8.

3. *The Borderers*, II, 782–5, 958 ff. Cf. *Fragment*, ll. 157–60, 205–11.

marked the stag's dying leap, only the fountain cupped with stone where no living creature will now drink. In time "These monuments shall all be overgrown." [4] In *Address to Kilchurn Castle, upon Loch Awe,* though the castle is the "Child of loud-throated War," its "fierce beginnings," "the strife, / The pride, the fury uncontrollable" are lost in the distance of time. The castle itself belongs to the "unknown modes of being":

> Oh! there is life that breathes not; Powers there are
> That touch each other to the quick in modes
> Which the gross world no sense hath to perceive,
> No soul to dream of.

The castle is the impersonation of time's "memorial majesty"; it is the "Shade of departed power." [5] Behind it rises Mt. Cruachan, about it are the waters of Loch Awe—and the castle, the life that breathes not, rules the scene.

Though Kilchurn Castle seems detached from the war and violence that once surrounded it, in *The White Doe* the ruin of Rylstone, the mansion and the pleasant bowers that perish along with the family, once again links structure with mortal disasters. The "hoary pile / Subdued by outrage and decay" [6] is by contrast with the white doe a child of time; the powers which the gross world cannot perceive now center not in the structure but in the spiritualized doe. In the later poetry the ruined structure tends to merge with the religious structure and to be softened by the healing growths of Nature. The silence of Nature has settled over the ruins of Fort Fuentes; there the lizard and the green, gilded snake and the bird now dwell, the "whirlwind of human destruction" long since spent. [7] Time itself is called kind in the sonnet *Composed among the Ruins of a Castle in North Wales,* but more usually time is the destroyer and Nature the healer. [8] The sense of man's own destructiveness lingers, for time and man together have wrought the ruins. The ruined structures in the later poetry are, however, for the most part simply occasions for description or meditation. [9]

Margart's ruined cottage in Book I of *The Excursion* is at once a ruined and a domestic structure. Its antecedent lies in the previously men-

---

4. Ll. 125–36, 176. See also *Inscriptions*, VII, in which the mere invasion of Nature's peace is regarded as an outrage.
5. Ll. 1, 6–9, 20–1, 31, 40–2.
6. Ll. 1905–6.
7. *Fort Fuentes*, stanzas 2, 3, 5.
8. See *Among the Ruins of a Convent in the Apennines* and *At Furness Abbey*.
9. See *Iona* (On to Iona!), *Among the Ruins of a Convent in the Apennines*, and *At Furness Abbey*. Wordsworth's tendency simply to describe and reflect on an artistic structure, ruined or otherwise, accounts for the frequent poems describing paintings, sculptures, etc. See *Monument of Mrs. Howard; The Last Supper, by Leonardo da Vinci; The Column Intended by Buonaparte for a Triumphal Edifice in Milan, Now Lying by the Way-Side in the Simplon Pass; The Pillar of Trajan,* etc.

tioned hut of *Incipient Madness;* like that hut the state of Margaret's cottage is the objective correlative of her increasing misery. When the Poet meets the Wanderer near it after Margaret's death it is roofless, "four naked walls / That stared upon each other." The garden wall is broken, the well half choked, the garden full of matted weeds.[1] The spot speaks to the Wanderer of mortality and mutability:

> we die, my Friend,
> Nor we alone, but that which each man loved
> And prized in his peculiar nook of earth
> Dies with him, or is changed; and very soon
> Even of the good is no memorial left.[2]

The Wanderer's story of Margaret's slow heart-wasting develops as much through the description of the slow decay of her cottage and garden as through description of Margaret herself.

Interestingly enough, almost the only other dwellings that similarly image the state of the inhabitant appear in the rest of *The Excursion.*[3] The description of the Solitary's dwelling certainly gives an image of much of his way of life. The dwelling, which from a distance had appeared fair, close by has a "forbidding nakedness"; within, the house is silent except for the mournful ticking of the solitary clock. The Solitary's apartment is "dark and low," cluttered "With books, maps, fossils, withered plants and flowers; / And tufts of mountain moss." Tools and papers lie mixed on the floor; a broken angling rod and a broken telescope, both covered with dust, are in a corner; unfinished and discarded musical instruments hang on the walls.[4] The state of the room quite clearly represents the state of the Solitary's mind.

The final domestic structure of *The Excursion* is the Pastor's. This too has its antecedents in Wordsworth's early poetry, where the cottage seems to be the image of the heart's desire.[5] The Pastor's home is no cottage but it similarly represents an ideal state. When the Wanderer, Solitary, and Poet, descending from the Solitary's lonely valley, first

1. Ll. 30–1, 453–62; Notes, *PW, 5,* 389, MS B, ll. 312–21.
2. Ll. 470–4. See Marian Mead, "The Happiest-Looking Homes of Men," in *Four Studies in Wordsworth* (Menasha, Wis., George Banta, 1929), p. 229. Mead points out that Wordsworth saw the house as "a sort of outer body of man, less sentient, slower in responding to the changes of his life, but still a part of his being, moulded by his spirit, flourishing with his welfare, and falling away with his decay."
3. Michael's cottage, known as the Evening Star, perhaps helps reveal the industrious life he and his family led; the lovely cottage that the reader of *Admonition* is told not to covet but to leave sacred to the poor perhaps images indirectly the life of its owners.
4. II, 640–71.
5. See above, p. 37, *Anacreon,* in which "The Cot, the seat of Peace and Love, / Peeping through the tufted grove" serves as a sexual image. See also *An Evening Walk* (1793), ll. 413–22, where the longed-for object that hope gilds for the poet across the dark gulf of time is the cottage that he hopes to share with Dorothy. In *Descriptive Sketches* (1793), ll. 724–39, the good life in Freedom's domain is imaged by the cottage with its neat pathway, its weedless garden, its humming bees, its clean supper board.

glimpse it, the Pastor's stately house looks like the dwelling of "A rural lord." Seen at close hand the house, like the church, is an "image of solemnity," "a reverent pile." With its pillared porch, mullioned windows, and fretted cornice, the house, set in the midst of flowers and shrubs and stately trees, has a "consummate harmony serene / Of gravity and elegance." [6] The dignity and well-ordered proportions of the parsonage again clearly symbolize the harmony and rightness of the Pastor's life. [7]

Most of the other structures that Wordsworth describes at length are religious structures. The religious structure in its first appearance is also ruined: one of the most terrible images in Wordsworth is that of the deserted chapel on the rocks in *The Borderers* whose bell, ringing in the wind, summons Herbert to his forsaken death. No other ruined religious structure has the dreadful implications of this chapel: the shapeless heap of stones that remains from St. Herbert's cell is regarded with reverence in memory of St. Herbert and his love for St. Cuthbert; [8] the ruined abbey of St. Mary where the invisible bird sang still offers repose and quietness. [9] The religious structure, however, is not characteristic of Wordsworth's early vision of reality; there the images are not static but vital. The period of the *Lyrical Ballads, The Prelude,* and the *Poems* of 1807 offers little by way of concrete structures. [1]

Peele Castle, which is of course not a religious structure, may perhaps be included here as showing how the architectural structure that was at first associated with evil and destruction moved toward the religious structure, symbol of permanence. In Beaumont's painting the violence is the violence of the storm beating upon the castle; the castle itself endures. "Cased in the unfeeling armour of old time," it stands sublimely braving lightning, wind, and waves. Wordsworth praises the painting, though it contrasts with his memory of the scene, and welcomes it as a sight "of what is to be borne!" [2] Clearly the architectural image is here moving away from mutability toward permanence.

The religious structure is a frequent vehicle in the poetry that followed *The Excursion.* The church that Poet, Wanderer, and Solitary enter in Book v of *The Excursion* is the first of these sacred piles, "for duration built." [3] They are all, of course, "Types of the spiritual Church." [4] Wordsworth is seeking "The house that cannot pass away"; [5]

6. v, 98; VIII, 450–90, 538–40.
7. See also v, 670–837.
8. *Inscriptions,* xv, *For the Spot Where the Hermitage Stood on St. Herbert's Island, Derwent Water.*
9. *The Prelude,* II, 102–28.
1. See, however, *The Prelude,* VI, A², the description of the convent of Chartreuse, based on *Descriptive Sketches* (1793), ll. 54–79.
2. *Elegiac Stanzas, Suggested by a Picture of Peele Castle,* ll. 49–52, 58.
3. v, 138, 145.
4. *Ecclesiastical Sonnets,* Pt. III, XLII, 2.
5. *Miscellaneous Sonnets,* Pt. III, XXVIII, 14.

if the physical structure is also a ruined one it does not much matter, for
the soul is reminded of heaven.[6] Graveyards move the mind heaven-
ward just as the church does; the poet is content "From pastoral graves
extracting thoughts divine." [7] Against the impermanence of human existence, in which "all things swerve / From their known course, or vanish like a dream," against "that transient Thing, / The human Soul,"
the church reminds man that his is not "a perishable home." [8]

The sonnet *Composed in Roslin Chapel during a Storm* links the religious structure with the life of nature. The poet listens to the wind and
marks the herbs growing in the now disused chapel among the sculptures,

> that, green-grown,
> Copy their beauty more and more, and preach,
> Though mute, of all things blending into one.

The sonnet *A Place of Burial in the South of Scotland* where the
church itself has vanished makes of the whole earth a church, for "neigh-
boring thickets ring / With *jubilate* from the choirs of spring." It is not
an altogether comforting idea, however, since the bereft who mourn in
that churchyard "in lowly anguish weep / Their prayers out to the wind
and naked skies." By and large it seems fair to say that in Wordsworth's
poetry after 1815 the religious structure tends to replace rather than
to merge with the life of nature.

Ruined structure, domestic structure, religious structure—the architectural image moves between the poles of mutability and permanence
and as domestic structure images the life of man. Except in *The Excursion,* architectural images are not usually dominant images: the ruin of
the Norton mansion images the perishable things of man set against the
imperishable things of the spirit. Metaphorical river and literal religious
structure combine in the *Ecclesiastical Sonnets* to image the imperishable. Even in that sequence, however, literal structure is tainted with
mortality. "The tower sublime / Of yesterday" that drops before "the
unimaginable touch of Time" [9] is the image of mutability.

Architectural metaphors and similes like water metaphors and similes
reinforce and make explicit the architectural symbols. Mansions and
temples are the kinds of structures that appear most frequently and they
are employed to emphasize permanence more often than mutability.[1]
Even in the great decade when Wordsworth saw into the life of things,
he simultaneously saw nature as a temple wherein man might wor-

6. *The Church of San Salvador, Iona* (On to Iona!).
7. *The River Duddon,* XXXI, 11. This seems a description of much of *The Excursion.*
8. *Ecclesiastical Sonnets,* Pt. I, XII, 9–10; XVI, 8–9; Pt. III, XLV, 1.
9. Pt. III, XXXIV, 10–11, 14.
1. For images of mutability see *The Prelude,* III, 428–30; *Composed after a Journey
across the Hambleton Hills, Yorkshire; The Excursion,* V, 589–90; *Malham Cove,* ll.
10–11; and *Inscriptions,* XI.

ship. The four great trees of Borrowdale make a natural temple; Wordsworth's own garden was a

> rocky corner in the lowest stair
> Of that magnificent temple which doth bound
> One side of our whole vale with grandeur rare.[2]

This way of seeing nature is dominant in *The Excursion* and frequent in the late poetry. The Solitary's sky vision is the most memorable of the architectural images of *The Excursion,* but natural surroundings are constantly imaged in architectural terms.[3] The rocks of *The Pass of Kirkstone* look like

> Altars for Druid service fit;
> (But where no fire was ever lit,
> Unless the glow-worm to the skies
> Thence offer nightly sacrifice)
> Wrinkled Egyptian monument;
> Green moss-grown tower; or hoary tent;
> Tents of a camp that never shall be razed—
> On which four thousand years have gazed![4]

The stars are mansions and

> All that we see—is dome, or vault, or nest,
> Or fortress, reared at Nature's sage command.[5]

Man himself is less often imaged in structural terms, though since the body is the abode of the soul [6] structural images are not unnatural. When Wordsworth resolves to write of humble folk, he remarks

> How oft high service is performed within,
> When all the external man is rude in show,—
> Not like a temple rich with pomp and gold,
> But a mere mountain chapel, that protects
> Its simple worshippers from sun and shower.[7]

The prophetic spirit of poetry has

> A metropolitan temple in the hearts
> Of mighty Poets.

2. *Yew-Trees,* l. 29; *A Farewell,* ll. 2–4. See also *The Prelude,* vi, 741–3; *The Recluse,* ll. 618, 623–4; and "It is a beauteous evening."

3. ii, 824–76. Cf. iii, 714, where the Solitary mentions having seen the French Revolution as a golden palace rising. For nature in architectural terms see iii, 50 ff., 74, 101–6, 471–2; iv, 34 ff., 1156–87; ix, 499–502.

4. Ll. 13–20.

5. "The stars are mansions built by Nature's hand," ll. 7–8. See also "Mark the concentred hazels that enclose," ll. 11–14; *To Dora,* ll. 35–9; and *The Wild Duck's Nest.*

6. *Ecclesiastical Sonnets,* Pt. i, xvi, 9–10. See also *The Excursion,* v, 588–9.

7. *The Prelude,* xiii, 227–31.

The mind as well as the heart lends itself to architectural images, frequently being termed a mansion.[8] The insights of the mind, poetic activity, and faith itself are presented in architectural terms.[9]

Like the water images architectural images appear throughout the entire range of Wordsworth's poetry. The early architectural figures link desolation and decay with man's imperfection; the later architectural images make of nature and man temples of the spirit. Architectural figures and water figures would seem to be incompatible but in actuality are not:[1] the mansions of poetry are bright, liquid mansions and the river of faith leads to the eternal city. Water images, however, are predominant in *The Prelude* and architectural images are infrequent; the proportions are reversed in *The Excursion*. While water imagery dominates, the sense of life is strong; where architectural images dominate, there is inevitably less movement and less life. Architectural images are by nature static; the more nature is a temple, the less it is alive.

Sounds, waters, and structures are to my mind secondary images, lesser motifs that mix with the dominant themes of landscape and solitary wanderer. Sounds tend to symbolize the unseen and spiritual; waters symbolize life, primarily that of feeling and thought; structures symbolize the perishability of mortal power, glory, and empire and the permanence of the city of the soul. In these images Wordsworth's mind moved between the poles of life and death, time and eternity, mutability and permanence. They reveal once again his use of the immediate and actual to realize both the subjective and the transcendent; they also reveal in the later poetry his increasing tendency to read the universe not as a showing forth of the divine but as apart from the divine.

8. Prospectus to *The Excursion*, ll. 86–7. See *Ecclesiastical Sonnets*, Pt. II, xxx, 12; *The Prelude*, IV, 339–43; VIII, A, 469–70; and *Tintern Abbey*, ll. 139–40.
9. See *The Prelude*, VII, 650–2; II, 376–86, 277–81; III, 619–31; *The Excursion*, VIII, 21 ff.; *The Prelude*, I, A, 127–31; V, 600–1, 22 ff.; *Inscriptions*, IV, *For a Seat in the Groves of Coleorton*, ll. 19–20; "In my mind's eye a Temple, like a cloud."
1. See *A Night-Piece*.

VI

A Chilled Age

THE limitations of Wordsworth's achievement have already been touched upon. He failed to write the great philosophic poem that he wished to write. The late poetry, despite its recent defenders,[1] has lost the glory and the dream. Why Wordsworth ceased writing great poetry is a question largely outside the scope of this study;[2] a few relevant observations may, however, be made.

Wordsworth's best poetry is autobiographical, giving his imaginative response to certain persons and places. In *The Prelude* he describes his own breakdown and recovery in personal terms; in *The Excursion* he attempts to generalize the experience and, in the Wanderer's prescription for the Solitary, to point the way back to health for men in general. The attempt to generalize the experience, to escape the limitations of the purely personal, was not a success. Is it then, as James seems to suggest,[3] that Wordsworth's kind of imagery was suited only for personal poetry, that when he attempted to broaden his base the images of men and landscape were no longer adequate tools?

To a certain extent this is true. One sets *Paradise Lost* against *The Excursion* and recognizes that had Wordsworth been able to integrate the personal with the traditional in a comparable fashion he might have achieved his philosophic poem.[4] But then one remembers *The Divine*

1. See especially Mary E. Burton, *The One Wordsworth* (Chapel Hill, University of North Carolina Press, 1942) and Edith C. Batho, *The Later Wordsworth* (New York, Macmillan, 1933).

2. The failure seems to me fundamentally a question for the biographer. A rather unstable person as a boy—see Meyer, *Wordsworth's Formative Years*—Wordsworth achieved a favorable issue from one period of introversion, releasing energies that produced the poetry of the glorious decade. (On the problem of introversion and its outcome see Herbert Silberer, *Problems of Mysticism and Its Symbolism*, tr. Jelliffe [New York, Moffat, Yard, 1917], pp. 307 ff.) Subjected to further shock in the deaths of his brother and children, finding Coleridge a burden rather than an inspiration, Wordsworth was unable to retain the equilibrium he had achieved, the personality hardened, the energies ebbed. See Harper, *William Wordsworth, 1,* 6–7; *2,* 128 ff.

3. James, *The Romantic Comedy,* p. 87, finds that Wordsworth's poetry "combines greatness and purity in the highest degree, when . . . he beheld men and landscapes in a symbolical way." James implies that Wordsworth's limitation lies in his inability to employ myth.

4. Basil Willey, "'Nature' in Wordsworth," *The Eighteenth Century Background* (London, Chatto & Windus, 1940), pp. 285–6, regards the "semi-Platonic machinery of pre-existence, reincarnation, and recollection" of the *Intimations* ode as a myth which enabled Wordsworth "to embody his experience objectively, and elevate it to a degree of impersonality normally beyond his reach."

Comedy in which Dante uses images of persons and places for the richest and most cómplex vision in poetry. Wordsworth should, one thinks, have been able to use his customary tools, his images of men and landscapes, for a great poem. What then was the trouble?

One returns to one's comparison of *The Excursion* with *Paradise Lost* and *The Divine Comedy* and the answer becomes simply that there was in Wordsworth a failure of the image-making capacity. The failure of *The Excursion* springs less from the limitations of Wordsworth's kind of imagery than from a failure of imagination. Milton in the figure of Satan presents an image of unyielding pride and in the degeneration of Satan an image of the outcome of such pride in dust and ashes. Dante not only presents the damned through images but in his own journey presents an image of the soul's journey to salvation—the recognition and rejection of evil, the ascent into grace. Wordsworth fails in *The Excursion* to present comparable images which *contain* the ideas. The Solitary's dwelling gives a partial image of the Solitary's confused and purposeless existence, but there is no further image.[5] The poem is static; it is all talk. Dante did not make the comparable mistake of having Vergil lecture him; *The Divine Comedy* has the showing forth in images that Wordsworth's poem should have had and lacks.

I have already said [6] that in my opinion the key to Wordsworth's later degeneration can be seen in his use in Margaret's story of the weeds and spear grass as a reconciling image. The original title for Margaret's story was *The Ruined Cottage*. The roofless hut itself, its four bare walls, its garden overgrown with weeds, in the midst of the bare open moorland, was Wordsworth's original image; it should be central to the poem, like Michael's uncompleted sheepfold or like the thorn. Like them the ruined cottage gives a vision of human sorrow and suffering that had somehow been endured; its beauty should come like theirs from the human feelings experienced there. But the Wanderer, looking at the weeds and spear grass about the cottage, tells us that once when he had passed them silvered over with raindrops they had conveyed to him

> So still an image of tranquillity,
> So calm and still, and looked so beautiful
> Amid the uneasy thoughts which filled my mind,
> That what we feel of sorrow and despair

5. Possibly Margaret's ruined cottage and the Pastor's mansion can be regarded as framework for the central section dealing with the Solitary: Margaret's cottage is a place sanctified by her love and loyalty, and the Pastor's mansion, linked by its path to the church, set among trees and flowers, graced by its radiant girl and godly matron, pictures an ideal existence. Both contrast with the Solitary's cottage which in its forbidding nakedness and in the wreck and jumble of its interior seems the image of a life that is indeed lost. Yet the pictures are curiously detached from each other and unrelated to any action.

6. See above, p. 61.

From ruin and from change, and all the grief
That passing shows of Being leave behind,
Appeared an idle dream.[7]

When feelings become an idle dream, poetry ceases to be possible. The philosophizing mind in adding the image of tranquillity is denying the wellsprings of poetry. This is not to say that the philosophizing mind is not to be desired in poetry. It is to say that philosophy *at the price of feeling* is not to be desired in poetry. Wordsworth's own theory makes the interconnection of the feelings and the imagination clear. Evidently when he denied his feelings the imagination suffered too.

The consequences of the growth of the philosophic mind at the expense of feeling can be seen in at least two ways in Wordsworth. I have already commented on the splitting of his image pattern, whereby light and life and love went out of this world. Increasingly in the later poetry the universe was not a showing forth of the divine but was apart from the divine. Similarly the solitary wanderer became a Solitary and a Wanderer, and thereafter there was little significant vision of human beings. The difficulty, I suggest, is not so much the shifting of Wordsworth's tenor from immanent to transcendent divinity as in the accompanying loss of interest in the human mind and human being. Milton and Dante both wrote of transcendent divinity but their poems will also read as studies in the way of the soul. In Satan and in Adam, Milton presents the negative and the positive reaction to sin; in Dante's descent into hell Dante presents, as Dorothy Sayers has observed in her new translation, not only traditional views on the nature of sin but also a study of the subjective hardening into sin. Had Wordsworth similarly integrated his later belief in "transcendent truths / Of the pure intellect" [8] with comparable insight into the human psyche, his poetry would, I think, have remained alive. Wordsworth, however, in *The Excursion* seems at cross purposes with himself: his aim is the healing of the Solitary; the Wanderer at moments stresses the importance of capacity for feeling and principally the importance of love; [9] yet in the steady focus upon eternity and in the suggestion that the earth and everyone in it shall pass away [1] Wordsworth tends to minimize the importance of any human life. His poetry has turned away from the mind of man, away from human feelings, in the direction of the *Ecclesiastical Sonnets*.

The growth of the philosophic mind at the expense of feeling appears not only in the change in Wordsworth's center of interest but also in the altered nature of his imagery. Where the concrete had been cen-

---

7. *The Excursion*, I, 946–52.
8. *The Excursion*, IV, 96–7.
9. IV, 611 ff., 1207 ff.
1. See above, pp. 49–50, and *The Excursion*, IV, 100 ff.

tral it became secondary. Wordsworth really describes what happened
to himself when he describes the difficulties of his age:

> yet we, who now
> Walk in the light of day, pertain full surely
> To a chilled age, most pitiably shut out
> From that which *is* and actuates, by forms,
> Abstractions, and by lifeless fact to fact
> Minutely linked with diligence uninspired,
> Unrectified, unguided, unsustained,
> By godlike insight.[2]

In Wordsworth's great poetry, abstractions are *actuated* by forms
and images. The

> Wisdom and Spirit of the universe!
> Thou Soul, that art the Eternity of thought!
> And giv'st to forms and images a breath
> And everlasting motion!

appears behind the solitary cliffs that wheel by the skater who has stopped
short,

> even as if the earth had rolled
> With visible motion her diurnal round![3]

Eventually abstractions were not actuated by forms but only illustrated
and there was much lifeless fact.

One image which appears in three separate poems so illuminates
Wordsworth's apprenticeship, mastery, and decline that it may be
profitable to trace its development, even though extensive quotation will
be necessary. The image is that of a man on a mountain top listening to
the sound of waters below. It first appears in *Descriptive Sketches* with
no significance beyond that of literal description.

> —'Tis morn: with gold the verdant mountain glows,
> More high, the snowy peaks with hues of rose.
> Far stretch'd beneath the many-tinted hills,
> A mighty waste of mist the valley fills,
> A solemn sea! whose vales and mountains round
> Stand motionless, to awful silence bound.
> A gulf of gloomy blue, that opens wide
> And bottomless, divides the midway tide.
> Like leaning masts of stranded ships appear

2. *Musings near Aquapendente,* ll. 323–30.
3. *Influence of Natural Objects in Calling Forth and Strengthening the Imagination in Boyhood and Early Youth,* ll. 1–4, 59–60.

The pines that near the coast their summits rear
Of cabins, woods, and lawns a pleasant shore
Bounds calm and clear the chaos still and hoar;
Loud thro' that midway gulf ascending, sound
Unnumber'd streams with hollow roar profound.
Mounts thro' the nearer mist the chaunt of birds,
And talking voices, and the low of herds,
The bark of dogs, the drowsy tinkling bell,
And wild-wood mountain lutes of saddest swell.
Think not, suspended from the cliff on high
He looks below with undelighted eye.[4]

De Selincourt has called attention to the fact that this image is essentially that developed in the description of the view from Mt. Snowdon. This description is so well known that I shall quote only the lines in which Wordsworth gives significance to the scene.

A meditation rose in me that night
Upon the lonely Mountain when the scene
Had pass'd away, and it appear'd to me
The perfect image of a mighty Mind,
Of one that feeds upon infinity,
That is exalted by an underpresence,
The sense of God, or whatsoe'er is dim
Or vast in its own being, above all
One function of such mind had Nature there
Exhibited by putting forth, and that
With circumstance most awful and sublime,
That domination which she oftentimes
Exerts upon the outward face of things,
So moulds them, and endues, abstracts, combines,
Or by abrupt and unhabitual influence
Doth make one object so impress itself
Upon all others, and pervade them so
That even the grossest minds must see and hear
And cannot chuse but feel. The Power which these
Acknowledge when thus moved, which Nature thus
Thrusts forth upon the senses, is the express
Resemblance, in the fulness of its strength
Made visible, a genuine Counterpart

4. 1793 text, ll. 492–511. This image was taken by Wordsworth from Ramond de Carbonnières's translation, *Lettres de M. William Coxe à M. W. Melmoth, sur l'état politique, civil et naturel de la Suisse; traduites de l'anglais, et augmentées des observations faites dans le même pays, par le traducteur.* See *Wordsworth: Representative Poems,* ed. Beatty, p. 53, n. 56, and pp. 33–4. De Selincourt in *PW, 1,* 328, also calls attention to James Beattie, *Minstrel, 1,* xxi ff., as a source of this image.

And Brother of the glorious faculty
Which higher minds bear with them as their own.[5]

Scene and significance are here in equipoise; the moonlight on the mist and the sound of water rising are "the express resemblance" of the power of the mind to transform the external world. Though the meditation rises only after the scene has passed away, the concept originates in the concrete, gradually becoming explicit as the poet broods on the scene.

The same scene, though without the mist, appears once again in the Wanderer's discourse in *The Excursion*, Book IX. This I shall quote in its entirety:

"Rightly it is said
That Man descends into the VALE of years;
Yet have I thought that we might also speak,
And not presumptuously, I trust, of Age,
As of a final EMINENCE; though bare
In aspect and forbidding, yet a point
On which 'tis not impossible to sit
In awful sovereignty; a place of power,
A throne, that may be likened unto his,
Who, in some placid day of summer, looks
Down from a mountain-top,—say one of those
High peaks, that bound the vale where now we are.
Faint, and diminished to the gazing eye,
Forest and field, and hill and dale appear,
With all the shapes over their surface spread:
But, while the gross and visible frame of things
Relinquishes its hold upon the sense,
Yea almost on the Mind herself, and seems
All unsubstantialized,—how loud the voice
Of waters, with invigorated peal
From the full river in the vale below,
Ascending! For on that superior height
Who sits, is disencumbered from the press
Of near obstructions, and is privileged
To breathe in solitude, above the host
Of ever-humming insects, 'mid thin air
That suits not them. The murmur of the leaves
Many and idle, visits not his ear:
This he is freed from, and from thousand notes
(Not less unceasing, not less vain than these,)
By which the finer passages of sense

5. *The Prelude*, XIII, A, 66–90.

> Are occupied; and the Soul, that would incline
> To listen, is prevented or deterred.
>
> "And may it not be hoped, that placed by age
> In like removal, tranquil though severe,
> We are not so removed for utter loss;
> But for some favour, suited to our need?
> What more than that the severing should confer
> Fresh power to commune with the invisible world,
> And hear the mighty stream of tendency
> Uttering, for elevation of our thought,
> A clear sonorous voice, inaudible
> To the vast multitude; whose doom it is
> To run the giddy round of vain delight,
> Or fret and labour on the Plain below.[6]

Here the scene is not primary but illustrative of an idea. Age is an eminence from which one hears the mighty stream of tendency—the real man on the real mountain listening to a real sound has become imaginary. The abstraction is not actuated by the form and image; it is only illustrated.

By 1833 Wordsworth was able to write the sonnet "Most sweet it is with unuplifted eyes" in which the traveler forbears to look at the region around him, being preoccupied by "some soft ideal scene" of the mind. Thought and love are the essentials, says Wordsworth:

> With Thought and Love companions of our way,
> Whate'er the senses take or may refuse,
> The Mind's internal heaven shall shed her dews
> Of inspiration on the humblest lay.

In Wordsworth's dream [7] the Arab fled the rising waters, carrying the book and the shell. Wordsworth himself seems to have fled from the living world of the senses and feelings to the dead world of abstraction and lifeless fact. As long as the mind acted upon something the senses took, the waters of life sounded and continue to sound through the shell of Wordsworth's poetry. When metaphor and simile merely illustrated abstractions, when the feelings were denied, then the literal was not transfigured and the shell did not and does not sing.

6. *The Excursion,* IX, 48–92.
7. *The Prelude,* V, 71 ff.

VII

Wordsworth's Theory of Imagery

WORDSWORTH'S theory of imagery is almost inextricably linked with his general theories concerning poetry and language. Strange as it seems at this date, Wordsworth's general theory of poetry has as yet received no adequate attention; his theory of diction has been most competently studied, his ideas in their philosophical connections have been dealt with, his mind has been analyzed, but his theory of poetry has not been carefully studied. Certainly his theory of his art has not deserved such neglect. In 1831 John Stuart Mill wrote to John Sterling that no one could talk with Wordsworth about the theory of poetry without feeling that Wordsworth had made greater contributions to it than had any other man. In Mill's opinion Wordsworth was not only a great poet but a great theorist about the principles of poetry.[1] De Quincey acknowledged his obligation to his conversation with Wordsworth over many years not only for his famous distinction between the literature of knowledge and the literature of power but "for most of the sound criticism on poetry, or any subject connected with it that I have ever met with."[2]

Wordsworth's own essays and prefaces account in part for this neglect: no one of them in any way attempts a comprehensive survey of the theories by which his poems were written. At the beginning of the "Preface to the Second Edition of the Lyrical Ballads," which is sometimes treated as if it were a complete statement of Wordsworth's theory, Wordsworth specifically stated that a systematic defense of his theory would, if adequately treated, "require a space wholly disproportionate to a preface." He therefore limited himself to discussing only the most controversial aspects of his experimental poems—his choice of subject and of language together with his reasons for putting such subjects and such language into verse. The Appendix of 1802 made clear the sense in which he had used the phrase "poetic diction"; the "Preface to the Edition of 1815" explained Wordsworth's classification of his poems; the supplementary essay of 1815 seems primarily a defense of the lasting worth of his poems on the ground that poetry popular in its own day has often proved of no lasting value whereas great poetry has most often

1. *The Letters of John Stuart Mill*, ed. Hugh S. R. Elliot (London, Longmans, Green, 1910), *1*, 11–12.
2. Thomas De Quincey, "Letters to a Young Man," *The Collected Writings of Thomas De Quincey*, ed. David Mason (Edinburgh, A. & C. Black, 1890), *10*, 48, n.

been at first neglected. Neither from any one of these essays nor from all of them put together can Wordsworth's theory of poetry be reconstructed. The critic must put with them passages from Wordsworth's letters, from his essays on epitaphs, from conversations preserved in the records of his friends, and, above all, from *The Prelude*. Only then does his thinking on poetry, language, and imagery emerge in all its interrelations.

The scattered nature of Wordsworth's remarks is further complicated by the fact that Wordsworth seldom if ever clearly differentiated figurative imagery from "language" and by the fact that he made his most penetrating remarks on imagery while talking about the imagination. Nevertheless, no sensitive reader of *The Prelude* can doubt that Wordsworth had done long and deep thinking about his art or that he had arrived at ideas about it that are worth our attention.

I shall attempt here only to state as clearly as I can what Wordsworth's ideas were. The full significance of his ideas about language, poetry, and imagery can be understood, however, only against the background of the philosophy of metaphor general in the eighteenth century. Therefore a brief survey of eighteenth-century philosophy of metaphor seems necessary as an introduction to our study of Wordsworth's own ideas.[3]

During the Restoration and the eighteenth century, philosophers and scientists regarded language as being atomic in structure, with each word referring to a single idea. Total meaning was regarded as simply the sum of the meanings of the individual word-atoms. The sole purpose of language was thought to be the communication of ideas: consequently an ideal language would have "a one-to-one correspondence between thing and word." Hartley compared words to the letters used in algebra and termed language a species of algebra.[4] In the seventeenth century the Royal Society had commissioned Bishop Wilkins to develop a language that would satisfy the scientists' ideal. Swift's conversationalists in the Academy of Lagado who carry about a packful of objects and silently point to them may exemplify the ridiculousness of the ideal of one-to-one correspondence of thing and word: the fact remains that this was the ideal of the century for language.[5]

Since each thing or idea had its proper name, metaphor was regarded as willful aberration, a calling of something that already had a name by some other name. It was simply the clothing of thought; the thought

3. In this discussion of eighteenth-century opinion I am for the most part summarizing and paraphrasing Scott George, "The Eighteenth Century Philosophy of Metaphor" (Ph.D. dissertation, Vanderbilt University, 1943). A summary of this dissertation has been distributed by the Joint University Libraries, Nashville, Tennessee, 1945. My references, however, are to the dissertation itself, to which I am greatly indebted.

4. David Hartley, *Observations on Man, His Frame, His Duty, and His Expectations* (London, 1749), Pt. I, chap. iii, sec. I.

5. George, pp. 14–15, 37–42.

was believed to remain the same regardless of how the clothing altered.[6] The use of metaphor was believed to have originated from a lack of words in primitive times and from the pressure of emotion: language that was rational and exact would not use metaphors because there was no longer a shortage of words, and emotional transfer from vehicle to tenor falsified the tenor. Hobbes, Locke, Berkeley, and Hume were in complete agreement about the irrationality of metaphor. Locke's attack on "all the art of rhetoric . . . all the artificial and figurative application of words" as "perfect cheats" that do nothing but mislead the judgment may be taken as representative of the attitude.[7]

Such an attitude toward language and metaphor inevitably meant that the scientific-philosophic attitude toward poetry was at best one of amused tolerance. Poetry was thought to differ from prose only in form: it was simply meaning plus ornament. As such it lacked validity, for metaphor robbed it of scientific exactness. Hume's remark "that the least reflection dissipates the illusions of poetry, and places the object in its proper light" indicates the status of poetry. Most of the beauties of poetry Hume believed to be founded "on falsehood and fiction." [8]

The eighteenth-century defenders of poetry attempted to make metaphor and poetry intellectually respectable in the face of the philosophic attack. Accepting the assumption that metaphor was essentially an ornament which left the nature of the idea being expressed unchanged, the apologists for poetry justified metaphor as being useful as well as ornamental. Pope's famous comparison in *An Essay on Criticism* of the "heights of Arts" to the endless ranges of the Alps [9] won Dr. Johnson's praise for both illustrating and ennobling the subject.[1] According to Blair, figures make a subject clearer and more striking;[2] according to Addison, the chief design of an allusion is "to illustrate and explain the passages of an author." [3] "The idea of an ornament admits use, though it seems to exclude necessity," wrote Dr. Johnson.[4]

Metaphor, according to its defenders, in addition to being useful was pleasant. The human mind takes a natural pleasure in finding resemblance, a pleasure which metaphor gratifies. But it affords not merely the intellectual gratification of this discovery but the further gratifica-

6. See James Harris, *Philological Inquiries in Three Parts* (London, 1781), Pt. II, chap. x.
7. John Locke, *An Essay concerning Human Understanding,* ed. Alexander C. Fraser (Oxford, Clarendon Press, 1894), *2,* 146–7.
8. *David Hume, Treatise of Human Nature, the Philosophical Works of David Hume* (Edinburgh, 1826), *1,* 168.
9. Ll. 219–32.
1. Samuel Johnson, "Pope," *Lives of the English Poets* (World's Classics, London, Oxford University Press, 1938), *2,* 328–9.
2. Hugh Blair, *Lectures on Rhetoric and Belles Lettres* (London, 1787), *1, 362.*
3. *The Spectator,* No. 421.
4. *The Rambler,* No. 139.

tion of introducing an inherently attractive object. Addison terms this "the pleasure of the imagination" and recommends the selection of the vehicle from pleasing objects. A vehicle employing an ugly object can please simply by showing a resemblance; however, a vehicle employing an object that is intrinsically sublime or beautiful gives not only the pleasure of the resemblance but in addition gives pleasure in and of itself.[5] The poetic quality seems to inhere in beautiful or sublime objects, with which the poet will take care to adorn his poem. According to the doctrine of the association of ideas, a pleasing vehicle will render the tenor pleasing by association so that the original subject can be made to appear more agreeable than it really is.[6]

Finally, metaphor was defended as lending life and interest to intellectual subjects, since illustrations that appeal to the senses improve our interest in an abstract subject.[7] The particularity of the vehicle gives emotional force and energy to the tenor and renders it more interesting than it would be by itself. A poet by his allusions, says Addison, makes the imagination reflect a truth in the understanding: "we are able to see something like color and shape in a notion, and to discover a scheme of thoughts traced out upon matter."[8]

The writers of the century tended to regard each metaphor as a separate and independent beauty. Idea and image were thought of as being mechanically linked: the imagination suggested possible images for the idea, the reason selected those most valuable for illustration, and the taste finally approved the image most agreeable as well as useful. The image at best was associated by resemblance to the idea; the two had no necessary organic connection. Since the process was regarded as one of mechanical linkage, rules could be formulated for the inclusion and construction of metaphor. Ironically enough, the highest subjects were thought not to require metaphor: what is already sublime stands in no need of adornment. And the strongest expressions of emotion likewise were not thought to require metaphor: voluntary ornament is out of place with great passion. The logic of ornament excluded metaphor, the chief poetic ornament, from the truly sublime and the truly pathetic and reserved its use for the middle ground where the ornament might make up for the inherent poetic deficiencies of a subject that was not itself beautiful or sublime. Rules for the construction of metaphor advised the use of a familiar vehicle grounded on a similitude easy to understand but still fresh enough to be surprising.[9]

Obviously this account of eighteenth-century philosophy of metaphor

5. *The Spectator*, No. 418.
6. Henry Home, Lord Kames, *Elements of Criticism* (Edinburgh, 1762), I, 76.
7. James Beattie, "On Poetry and Music, as They Affect the Mind," *Essays* (Edinburgh, 1776), p. 337.
8. *The Spectator*, No. 421. See George, chap. iii, throughout; I have greatly condensed and somewhat reordered George's argument.
9. George, chaps. iv, v.

is greatly oversimplified.[1] But the essential points are simple enough. The philosophic thinkers of the century, hoping to attain a language that would serve the purposes of science in exact communication of ideas, frowned on the metaphor for introducing irrelevant and unrelated items into discourse. Valuing plain prose truth, such writers tended to regard poetry as simply a kind of ornamented prose and its figures as the poet's means of ornamenting. The defenders of poetry, having no other philosophy of language, accepted the basic assumption that metaphor was essentially ornament. The mechanistic philosophy underlies both the attacks on poetry and the defenses of it: the best a poet could do was to start with a subject and ornament it by associating it with naturally appealing objects.

It has sometimes been assumed that Wordsworth's ideas about imagery fundamentally resemble those of the eighteenth century. Cleanth Brooks, in his discussion of "Metaphor and the Tradition" in *Modern Poetry and the Tradition,* equates the theory and practice of Wordsworth and the Romantics in general with respect to metaphor with that of the eighteenth century. Brooks regards not only Wordsworth's own imagery but all Romantic metaphor as being like eighteenth-century imagery mere illustration and ornament; in his opinion the practice of both the eighteenth and the nineteenth centuries was based on the belief that certain words and subjects are intrinsically poetic and on antipathy to images that are intellectually difficult. Brooks says that Johnson's principles about imagery were "precisely those" of Wordsworth and Coleridge.[2] It is my purpose here to examine Wordworth's position in detail in the hope of reaching a rather more accurate statement of Wordsworth's theory of imagery.

Wordsworth in my opinion attacked the whole mechanistic philosophy,[3] including its view of poetry and imagery. The universe to Words-

---

1. Naturally there were dissident voices. The group most strongly disagreeing with the mechanistic philosophy and its corrolary literary theories was the group holding the idealistic philosophy. Looking to a higher reason than the naturalists would admit, the Platonists found value in poetry insofar as it became an allegory or symbol of the real. They wrote no defense of poetry or of metaphor, however, and seem to have had no great effect on literary theory.

2. Pp. 3–10.

3. There are two schools of thought concerning Wordsworth's philosophy. For an exposition that connects Wordsworth with the Locke-Hume-Hartley tradition, seeing his position as a development from the eighteenth-century English rationalists, the reader should consult Beatty, *William Wordsworth: His Doctrine and Art in Their Historical Relations.* The opposite position, emphasizing Wordsworth's mysticism and transcendentalism, appears in Havens, *The Mind of a Poet: A Study of Wordsworth's Thought with Particular Reference to the Mind of a Poet.* More balanced views are to be found in Melvin M. Rader, *Presiding Ideas in Wordsworth's Poetry,* University of Washington Publications in Language and Literature, 8, No. 2 (Seattle, 1931); in Newton P. Stallknecht, *Strange Seas of Thought* (Durham, Duke University Press, 1945); and in Joseph W. Beach, *The Concept of Nature in Nineteenth-Century English Poetry* (New York, Macmillan, 1936). Whitehead, *Science and the Modern World,* pp. 104–8, regards

worth was no mechanism but a living presence; the mind was no blank tablet but an active power. The same active life manifested itself in the world of nature and in the mind of man: when the outer and inner activities interacted, common reality was transfigured. The One Life is within us and abroad [4] and finds its most complete expression in poetry.

Much of Wordsworth's theory is clearly a reaction against the eighteenth-century derogation of poetry and a reassertion of poetry's claim to truth and dignity. Poetry is true: men who regard poetry as an amusement, who talk of a taste for poetry as if it were like a taste for ropedancing or sherry, simply do not know what they are talking about. The object of poetry is "truth . . . truth which is its own testimony, which gives strength and divinity to the tribunal to which it appeals, and receives them from the same tribunal. Poetry is the image of man and nature." [5] The fact that poetry must produce pleasure in no way degrades the poet's art. Scientists as well as poets build up their knowledge by means of pleasure; the knowledge of the scientist, however, separates him from other men instead of connecting him with them.

> The Man of science seeks truth as a remote and unknown benefactor; he cherishes and loves it in his solitude: the Poet, singing a song in which all human beings join with him, rejoices in the presence of truth as our visible friend and hourly companion. Poetry is the breath and finer spirit of all knowledge; it is the impassioned expression which is in the countenance of all Science. . . . Poetry is the first and last of all knowledge. [6]

When the discoveries of the scientist become familiar so that they arouse men's feelings, then these discoveries too will be material for the poet's art.

The famous distinction between the imagination and the fancy reinforces this insistence on the truthfulness of the highest poetry. Whatever in poetry was recognizably mere play, recognizably sheer invention, Wordsworth termed the work of the fancy. The fancy is willful; it distorts and invents, finding ghosts under yew trees, turning one visit of a widow to her husband's grave into never ending visits, seeing unhappy female vagrants reclining under drooping foxgloves; it is an

---

Wordsworth's "sense of the haunting presences of nature" as a philosophically sound criticism of the eighteenth-century mechanistic interpretation of reality. See also the discussion of Wordsworth's philosophy in Logan, *Wordsworthian Criticism: a Guide and Bibliography*, chap. vi.

4. See Coleridge, *The Eolian Harp*, l. 26. This line first appears in a passage added to the poem in 1817.

5. "Preface to the Lyrical Ballads," *PW*, 2, 394–5. "Strength and divinity" reads "competence and confidence" after 1836.

6. "Preface to the Lyrical Ballads," *PW*, 2, 396. Passage added in 1802.

"adulterate Power" whose shapes take value only as they are "grafted upon feelings / Of the imagination." [7] Fancy excites pleasure and surprise not by the individual value of images but by rapid variation and sheer number of images.[8] Wordsworth's distinction between fanciful and imaginative imagery is significant because it recognizes the existence of poetry that does not aspire to high truth and at the same time effectively opposes the idea that imagery is mere ornament.

The fancy may invent, it may serve the temporal man; the imagination reveals essential truth and supports the eternal.[9] The imagination deals "with objects not as they are, but as they appear to the mind of the poet"; [1] true vision develops as the mind contemplates the object. The poet will not make the mistake of seeing objects "as they exist in themselves," that is, "in disconnection dead and spiritless," [2] abstracted and isolated out from the world they belong in. The poet will treat of things as they exist to the senses and the passions; that is, he will restore them to wholeness, to their relationships and interconnections. True poetry is like religion in its dependence on words and symbols; it is "ethereal and transcendent, yet incapable to sustain her existence without sensuous incarnation." [3] The soul and essence of poetry—so Wordsworth said, according to the recollections of Aubrey de Vere—was "truth in its largest sense, as a thing at once real and ideal, a truth including exact and accurate detail, and yet everywhere subordinating mere detail to the spirit of the whole." [4]

The exact and accurate detail should in Wordsworth's opinion never be lost sight of. Flights into fancy away from the firm ground of reality were not for Wordsworth. The Prologue to *Peter Bell* embodies Wordsworth's rejection of anything but the known and the real. In his dedication to Southey, Wordsworth stated his belief that ordinary incidents of the most humble sort were proper material for the imagination. Rejecting the unknown, the strange, the supernatural, Wordsworth refused to soar in aerial heights, declaring his preference for "The common growth of mother-earth" and his belief that the poet could neither find nor create a nobler marvel than the human mind.[5] Wordsworth's notes dictated to Isabella Fenwick in 1843 repeatedly stressed the core of fact from which every poem had arisen—whether an ex-

7. *The Prelude*, VIII, A, 510–93; see also XIII, 289–306.
8. "Preface to the Edition of 1815," *PW*, *2*, 441. See also Wordsworth's note to *The Thorn, PW, 2,* 512.
9. "Preface to the Edition of 1815," *PW*, *2*, 441–2.
1. "Conversations and Reminiscences Recorded by the (Now) Bishop of Lincoln," *Prose Works, 3,* 464.
2. *The Excursion*, IV, 962.
3. "Essay, Supplementary to the Preface (1815)," *PW*, *2*, 410 ff.
4. *Prose Works, 3,* 488.
5. *Peter Bell*, ll. 131–50.

perience of his own, something related to him, or something of which he had read.[6]

Fact alone, however, does not produce the high truth of poetry; the mere fact must always be converted by the power of imagination into the higher truth of poetry. Therefore Wordsworth was dissatisfied with writers who seemed to him content with literal facts. Too many of Crabbe's pictures were "mere matters of fact: with which the Muses have just about as much to do as they have with a Collection of medical reports."[7] He felt readers would profit from contrasting Crabbe's matter-of-fact style with his own spiritualizing of the character in *Lucy Gray*. The fact that he threw "imaginative influences" over common life rendered the subject not less but more true.[8] His object in the poem had been to "exhibit poetically entire *solitude*"; the truth lay both in the detail of the child's seeing the moon at two in the afternoon and in the subordinating of detail to the total impression.[9] He defended the truth of an epitaph in which the character of the dead is idealized:

> The character of a deceased friend or beloved kinsman is not seen, no—nor ought to be seen, otherwise than as a tree through a tender haze or a luminous mist, that spiritualises and beautifies it; that takes away, indeed, but only to the end that the parts which are not abstracted may appear more dignified and lovely; may impress and affect the more. Shall we say then, that this is not truth, not a faithful image; and that accordingly, the purpose of commemoration cannot be answered?—It *is* truth, and of the highest order; for, though doubtless things are not apparent which did exist; yet, the object being looked at through this medium, parts and proportions are brought into distinct view which before had been only imperfectly or unconsciously seen: it is truth hallowed by love.[1]

"Common occurrences are transmuted into poetry";[2] the individual form is real and true and by the genius of the poet suggests not only literal truth but universal truth.[3]

Wordsworth's insistence on the truth of poetry should not mislead one into thinking that he regarded poetry as a didactic medium written to convey truths existing independent of the poetic, creative process. He wished, it is true, to be regarded as a teacher, and he seems some-

6. Legouis comments that Wordsworth so fully explained and justified his occasional changes in his facts that the changes seem less poetic inventions than scientific experiment. *The Early Life of William Wordsworth, 1770–1798*, tr. Matthews, p. 435.
7. *MY, 1,* 244.
8. *IF.*
9. *Diary, 2,* 24.
1. "Upon Epitaphs," *Prose Works, 2,* 36.
2. *Diary, 2,* 224.
3. *Diary, 2,* 25.

times to have mistaken the expression of opinion for poetry. But he knew the object of poetry to be "truth, not individual and local, but general, and operative; not standing upon external testimony, but carried alive into the heart by passion."[4] The words to be emphasized, I think, are "operative" and "alive." The poet must be equipped with "general truths," but these are no more than a sort

> Of Elements and Agents, Under-powers,
> Subordinate helpers of the living mind.[5]

The living mind must render the general truths vital and alive before they become poetry.

Only when the truth is alive so that it affects the heart is it poetry. Hence Wordsworth's emphasis upon passion in poetry. A primary requisite of an epitaph is that it have its basis in very ordinary thoughts and feelings, in everyday sensations and self-evident truths. "But it is required that these truths should be instinctively ejaculated or should rise irresistibly from circumstances; in a word that they should be uttered in such connection as shall make it felt that they are not adopted, not spoken by rote, but perceived in their whole compass with the freshness and clearness of an original intuition."[6] The "universally received truths" must be given a "pathos and spirit which shall re-admit them into the soul like revelations of the moment."[7] The commonplace must be restored to life.

Because truth must always be transformed by feeling into poetry, Wordsworth insisted that poetry originates only in the "spontaneous overflow of powerful feelings." Successful composition begins with "emotion recollected in tranquillity"—recollected until a kindred emotion is felt.[8] The "primary sensations of the human heart" are "the vital springs of sublime and pathetic composition" not only in epitaphs but in every kind of writing.[9] Wordsworth, being fully aware that one does not feel in a vacuum, that one always feels about something, was confident that in his own case feelings would always be connected with important subjects. Poetry required both "more than usual organic sensibility" and long and deep thinking.[1] Coleridge's letter to Poole of March 23, 1801, perhaps suggests the interrelationship most clearly: "deep thinking is obtainable only by a man of deep feeling, and . . . all truth is a species of revelation."[2] Truth, said Wordsworth, should be

4. "Preface to the Lyrical Ballads," *PW*, *2*, 394–5. Addition of 1802.
5. *The Prelude*, I, 152–3.
6. "Upon Epitaphs," *Prose Works*, *2*, 58.
7. "Upon Epitaphs," p. 63.
8. "Preface to the Lyrical Ballads," *PW*, *2*, 400–1.
9. "Upon Epitaphs," p. 48.
1. "Preface to the Lyrical Ballads," pp. 387–8.
2. *Letters of Samuel Taylor Coleridge*, ed. E. H. Coleridge, *1*, 351–2.

"a motion or a shape / Instinct with vital functions";[3] it is "the soul of passion."[4]

Poetic genius consisted, in Wordsworth's opinion, in extending the range of sensibility. He was not quite sure that he understood R. P. Gillies' position that every idea a poet has "may be made passionate, and therefore poetical." Wordsworth knew that the poet has many thoughts in common with other men and that many of them could never arouse poetic passion. But the real proof of genuine poetic genius, the real service a writer performs, is his work in calling forth and enlarging the capacity for feeling.[5] Every great and original author has had the task of *"creating* the taste by which he is to be enjoyed." The writer has to stir "a co-operating *power* in the mind of the Reader": the problem in overcoming custom and literary snobbery is the problem of "widening the sphere of human sensibility."[6]

Some of what to the cursory student of Wordsworth seems sheer didacticism is to be accounted for by this desire of his to extend the range of sensibility. One of Wordsworth's chief aims in *The Excursion* was "to put the commonplace truths, of the human affections especially, in an interesting point of view; and rather to remind men of their knowledge, as it lurks inoperative and unvalued in their own minds, than to attempt to convey recondite or refined truths."[7] He hoped, in other words, to make the knowledge *operative,* to make it power rather than knowledge. Were he not confident that his poems would "operate in their degree, to extend the domain of sensibility for the delight, the honour, and the benefit of human nature," he would not save them from destruction.[8] A great poet should do more than reflect faithfully "the feelings of human nature. . . . he ought, to a certain degree, to rectify men's feelings, to give them new compositions of feeling, to render their feelings more sane, pure, and permanent, in short, more consonant to nature, that is, to eternal nature, and the great moving spirit of things."[9]

Truth and passion, then, are essential to poetry. Wordsworth's meanings of both terms, however, can be really understood only as they are connected with his theory of imagination.

The imagination Wordsworth regarded as man's noblest faculty.[1] The word denoted "operations of the mind" upon objects and "processes of creation . . . governed by certain fixed laws."[2] The imagination is

3. *The Prelude,* VIII, 298–9.
4. "Upon Epitaphs," p. 70.
5. *MY, 2,* 614; see also "Preface to the Lyrical Ballads," p. 389.
6. "Essay, Supplementary to the Preface (1815)," *PW, 2,* 426–8.
7. *MY, 2,* 669.
8. "Essay, Supplementary to the Preface (1815)," p. 430.
9. *EL,* pp. 295–6.
1. "Essay, Supplementary to the Preface (1815)," p. 427.
2. "Preface to the Edition of 1815," *PW, 2,* 436.

that intellectual lens through the medium of which the poetical observer sees the objects of his observation, modified both in form and colour; or it is that inventive dresser of dramatic *tableaux,* by which the persons of the play are invested with new drapery, or placed in new attitudes; or it is that chemical faculty by which elements of the most different nature and distant origin are blended together into one harmonious and homogeneous whole.[3]

The power which Nature sometimes puts forth, when she "moulds,"

> endues, abstracts, combines,
> Or by abrupt and unhabitual influence
> Doth make one object so impress itself
> Upon all others, and pervade them so
> That even the grossest minds must see and hear
> And cannot chuse but feel.[4]

resembles the power the imagination has to transform the world. In other words the imagination is the creative, active life in the mind.[5]

[Wordsworth believed that the imagination is active in everyone in childhood. Love is the tie that links the newborn child to the universe in which he lives]

> Along his infant veins are interfused
> The gravitation and the filial bond
> Of nature that connect him with the world.

The "first / Poetic spirit of our human life" arises as the young baby feels his mother's love and responds to the world colored by that love.

3. "Conversations and Reminiscences Recorded by the (Now) Bishop of Lincoln," *Prose Works, 3,* 465.

4. *The Prelude,* xiii, A, 79–84.

5. Whether or not Wordsworth derived his belief in the creative activity of the mind from Kant by way of Coleridge or whether it was an intuitive conviction of his own, reinforced by conversation with Coleridge, seems unimportant. Since the creative activity of the mind is clearly stated in Books i and ii of *The Prelude,* which in De Selincourt's opinion were probably completed in the latter half of 1799 (p. xxxiv), before Coleridge had become well acquainted with Kant (see René Wellek, *Immanuel Kant in England, 1793–1838* [Princeton, Princeton University Press, 1931], pp. 69–72), it seems unnecessary to attribute the belief to Coleridge's influence. Certainly the writer who as a boy had had to take hold of external objects to remind himself of their existence (*IF* note to *Intimations* ode) did not need to derive his belief in the power of the mind from anyone. For discussion of Kant's possible influence on Wordsworth see Wellek, pp. 159–62, and Rader, *Presiding Ideas in Wordsworth's Poetry,* pp. 189–93. For discussion of the connection between Wordsworth's conception of the imagination and Kant's doctrine see Havens, *The Mind of a Poet,* pp. 205–7, and James, *Scepticism and Poetry: An Essay on the Poetic Imagination,* pp. 15–28.

Beatty, *William Wordsworth,* chap. viii, is of the opinion that even Wordsworth's belief in the creative power of the mind is derived from Hartley. Beatty seems to be forcing Hartley's theory of association considerably in identifying it with a belief in the creative activity of the mind. See Rader, chap. iii, who corrects Beatty's overemphasis of Wordsworth's debt to Hartley—though seeming in turn rather to overemphasize Wordsworth's debt to Coleridge.

> For feeling has to him imparted power
> That through the growing faculties of sense
> Doth like an agent of the one great Mind
> Create, creator and receiver both,
> Working but in alliance with the works
> Which it beholds.[6]

In most persons this creative, poetic spirit dies out under the deadening pressures of the workaday world.[7] When the world is too much with a man, he loses his visionary power. The years all too quickly bring "the inevitable yoke":

> Full soon thy Soul shall have her earthly freight,
> And custom lie upon thee with a weight,
> Heavy as frost, and deep almost as life![8]

Only too surely "use and custom" tend to submerge the soul and to deaden the inner life.[9]

Only "higher minds" succeed in retaining the creative life of the mind against the pressures of the world. The imaginative activity which rises in the child in response to love rightly leads on to a love higher than human love; minds in which this growth occurs are able to commune with the invisible. Imagination and spiritual insight become in Wordsworth's terms interchangeable;[1] imagination and intellectual love "are each in each, and cannot stand / Dividually." Such minds are responsive to the slightest stimulus; they live "in a world of life."

> Such minds are truly from the Deity,
> For they are Powers; and hence the highest bliss
> That flesh can know is theirs—the consciousness
> Of Whom they are, habitually infused
> Through every image and through every thought.

Wordsworth's own story as he tells it in *The Prelude* is a story of successful imaginative growth followed by

> lapse and hesitating choice,
> And backward wanderings along thorny ways.

At first the infant sensibility in him was not damped but sustained. He describes himself as having kept his soul unsubdued by the world.

---

6. *The Prelude*, II, 242–4, 255–60.
7. *The Prelude*, II, 260–3.
8. *Intimations* ode, ll. 130–2.
9. *The Prelude*, XIV, 157–62.
1. *The Prelude*, XIII, A, 165, 166–7: "This love more intellectual cannot be / Without Imagination." Final text reads "This spiritual Love acts not nor can exist / Without Imagination."

A plastic power
Abode with me; a forming hand, at times
Rebellious, acting in a devious mood;
A local spirit of his own, at war
With general tendency, but, for the most,
Subservient strictly to external things
With which it communed. An auxiliar light
Came from my mind, which on the setting sun
Bestowed new splendour; the melodious birds,
The fluttering breezes, fountains that run on
Murmuring so sweetly in themselves, obeyed
A like dominion, and the midnight storm
Grew darker in the presence of my eye.

The "auxiliar light" seems unquestionably the power of the imagination, called into activity and sustained by feeling.

Pain and fear were welcome to Wordsworth because they stirred this shaping power; throughout *The Prelude* he describes the way in which feelings made objects impress themselves upon his mind. To trace how this happened would be to rewrite *The Prelude*.

When his feelings were not deeply stirred, imagination slept. Wordsworth complains of this loss of the active power both when he writes of slipping into ordinary youthful activities at Cambridge and when he writes of the sights of Bartholomew Fair. The "perpetual whirl / Of trivial objects" Wordsworth found oppressive.[2]

The tendency to analyze and abstract, while a refuge from painful feelings, was for Wordsworth the greatest danger to the life of the imagination. In his depression he warred against himself, falling under the sway of the secondary reason, presumptuously analyzing and judging. The consequence of such analysis was once again the loss of imaginative power. From this trouble Wordsworth was redeemed by the strength of his early "Visitings of imaginative power"; his memories of the "spots of time" in his childhood when the mind had exerted its force enabled him to recover creative power. "The hiding-places" of his power lay in his childhood when the creative life of the mind had been strong; whenever wind or storm carried him back to those early moments the spirit once again worked within him.[3] When Wordsworth later lamented that "the earth, and every common sight" had lost the glory they had once had for him, that "the glory and the dream" had departed, he nevertheless rejoiced that there remained from childhood

Those shadowy recollections,
Which, be they what they may,

2. xiv, 208–9, 102–5, 112–16, 137–8; ii, 358–62, 362–74; iii, 237–61; vii, 678–81, 725–30.
3. xii, 44–151 (see xi, A, esp. 121–37), 201–7, 208–35. See also ii, 216–19.

Are yet the fountain-light of all our day,
Are yet a master-light of all our seeing.

Because of these recollections the "noisy years" would never completely subdue him.[4]

Wordsworth's own life story in *The Prelude* is the clearest evidence for his belief that the passions "build up our human soul." [5] Human passion is a "strong creative power"; [6] fear and love, most especially love, call forth the creative power.[7] Wordsworth's belief that it is feeling or passion which enables a poet to see an object imaginatively can also be inferred from his criticism of the poetry of the period intervening between *Paradise Lost* and *The Seasons:* it contained no new images from external nature "and scarcely presents a familiar one from which it can be inferred that the eye of the Poet had been steadily fixed upon his object, much less that his feelings had urged him to work upon it in the spirit of genuine imagination." [8]

If feeling is essential to stir the imagination, the imagination in its turn acts on the feelings. Wordsworth wrote Sir George Beaumont how he was walking through London early on a Sunday morning,

> when, looking up, I saw before me the avenue of Fleet Street, silent, empty, and pure white, with a sprinkling of new-fallen snow, not a cart or carriage to obstruct the view, no noise, only a few soundless and dusky foot-passengers here and there. You remember the elegant line of the curve of Ludgate Hill in which this avenue would terminate, and beyond, towering above it, was the huge and majestic form of St. Paul's, solemnised by a thin veil of falling snow. I cannot say how much I was affected at this unthought-of sight in such a place, and what a blessing I felt there is in habits of exalted imagination. My sorrow was controlled, and my uneasiness of mind—not quieted and relieved altogether—seemed at once to receive the gift of an anchor of security.[9]

Thus feeling and imagination were associated in Wordsworth's mind like two halves of a circle. Havens thinks that Wordsworth did "not mean that the composition of imaginative poems or passages is necessarily accompanied by strong emotion but that imaginative activity is possible only in natures capable of deep feeling." [1] On the contrary, I should think that Wordsworth meant what he said when he wished to

4. *Intimations* ode, ll. 153–6, 158.
5. *The Prelude,* I, 407.
6. *The Excursion,* I, 480.
7. *The Prelude,* XIV, 162 ff.
8. "Essay, Supplementary to the Preface (1815)," *PW, 2,* 419–20.
9. *MY, 1,* 186–7.
1. *The Mind of a Poet,* p. 217.

write "in truth / And sanctity of passion." [2] Poetry originated in emotion recollected in tranquillity so that time purged from it the accidental and the disfiguring; if it was good for anything, it appealed "forcibly to the imagination and the feelings." [3] Wordsworth was interested in works "of *imagination and sentiment*"; [4] the "enlightened Critic" looked in poetry "for a reflection of the wisdom of the heart and the grandeur of the imagination." [5] Disputed as this phrase has been,[6] the "wisdom of the heart" seems to refer to the intuitive wisdom which comes from both logic and feeling.[7] Wordsworth agreed with Dennis that poetic passion "is of two kinds; imaginative and enthusiastic, and merely human and ordinary." [8] Wordsworth intended his poetic passion to be imaginative, though that of his characters might be human and ordinary.

Wordsworth's theory of the imagination must also be correlated with his insistence on the truth of poetry. Imaginative power aroused by passion revealed, in Wordsworth's opinion, essential truth. The Wordsworth of the *Lyrical Ballads* seems at times to mistake psychological truth for imaginative truth. His principal object in those poems was

> to choose incidents and situations from common life, and to relate or describe them, throughout, as far as was possible in a selection of language really used by men, and, at the same time, to throw over them a certain colouring of imagination, whereby ordinary things should be presented to the mind in an unusual aspect; and, further, and above all, to make these incidents and situations interesting by tracing in them, truly though not ostentatiously, the primary laws of our nature: chiefly, as far as regards the manner in which we associate ideas in a state of excitement.[9]

2. *The Prelude*, XIII, 235–6.

3. *LY*, *2*, 650.

4. Appendix of 1802, *PW*, *2*, 409.

5. "Essay, Supplementary to the Preface (1815)," *PW*, *2*, 411.

6. See Brooks, *Modern Poetry and the Tradition*, p. 6, who reads the statement as evidence that Wordsworth believed the play of intellect to be "inimical to deep emotion," and also Pottle, *The Idiom of Poetry*, p. 51, who fears that "the statement means nothing very precise."

7. Cf. De Quincey, "The Poetry of Pope," *The Collected Writings of Thomas De Quincey*, *11*, 56: "It is in relation to those great *moral* capacities of man that the literature of power, as contradistinguished from that of knowledge, lives and has its field of action. It is concerned with what is highest in man; for the Scriptures themselves never condescended to deal by suggestion or co-operation with the mere discursive understanding: when speaking of man in his intellectual capacity, the Scriptures speak not of the understanding, but of *'the understanding heart'*—making the heart, *i.e.* the great *intuitive* (or non-discursive) organ, to be the interchangeable formula for man in his highest state of capacity for the infinite."

8. *MY*, *2*, 617.

9. "Preface to the Lyrical Ballads," *PW*, *2*, 386. Wording of ʳ802.

Here the "colouring of imagination" is virtually lost sight of in the interest in the primary laws of our nature. Wordsworth wrote *Peter Bell* in the belief that the imagination could be called forth by natural and humble incidents,[1] but the poem seems as much an investigation into psychology as an instance of "that infinity without which there is no poetry."[2] Similarly Wordsworth's long defense of the sonnet beginning "With Ships the sea was sprinkled far and nigh" seems based primarily on interest in the laws of the mind:

> There is scarcely one of my Poems which does not aim to direct the attention to some moral sentiment, or to some general principle, or law of thought, or of our intellectual constitution. For instance in the present case, who is there that has not felt that the mind can have no rest among a multitude of objects, of which it either cannot make one whole, or from which it cannot single out one individual, whereupon may be concentrated the attention divided among or distracted by a multitude? After a time we must either select one image or object, which must put out of view the rest wholly, or must subordinate them to itself while it stands forth as a Head.[3]

This interest in psychology is easy to understand. The imagination denotes "operations of the mind"; it is the inner activity that "can send abroad . . . mutations."[4] In Wordsworth himself "the fluxes and refluxes of the mind when agitated by the great and simple affections of our nature"[5] had often led to the visionary mood. Apparently Wordsworth found this consciousness of mental power—of creative power—so exciting that he considered any description of its activity to be poetry: there seems no other way of accounting for *Anecdote for Fathers* or *Goody Blake and Harry Gill.* Anything related to the action of the mind Wordsworth regarded as poetic.

Even more fundamentally, poetic truth blends into transcendental truth. [The imagination was to Wordsworth the noblest faculty of our nature because it is the eye of the soul. Recollections of moments of visionary power are precious because they keep alive within the soul the sense of other worlds than this one]

an obscure sense
Of possible sublimity, whereto
With growing faculties she doth aspire,
With faculties still growing, feeling still

1. Letter to Robert Southey, in *The Poetical Words of Wordsworth,* ed. Thomas Hutchinson (London, Oxford University Press, 1932), p. 236.
2. *Diary, 2,* 24.
3. *MY, I,* 128-9.
4. "Preface to the Edition of 1815," *PW, 2,* 436; *The Prelude,* xiv, 93-4.
5. "Preface to the Lyrical Ballads," *PW, 2,* 388, n.

That whatsoever point they gain, they yet
Have something to pursue.[6]

They keep alive the sense of worlds not realized, the high instincts [7]
which remind us that

Our destiny, our being's heart and home,
Is with infinitude, and only there;
With hope it is, hope that can never die,
Effort, and expectation, and desire,
And something evermore about to be.[8]

Although Wordsworth spoke of immediate reality as

the very world, which is the world
Of all of us,—the place where, in the end,
We find our happiness, or not at all! [9]

he quite definitely believed that we find our happiness here only as we
discover in the recesses of our natures our own creative powers.

Hence in his own poetry he most valued the spirituality with which
he had "endeavored to invest the material Universe, and the moral relation under which I have wished to exhibit its most ordinary appearances." [1] He defended *The White Doe of Rylstone* against Lamb's
criticism, pointing out that the poem was not likely to be popular because
the banner and doe were both imaginative agents and because all the
action was "fine-spun and inobtrusive . . . in harmony with the
shadowy influence of the Doe." Lamb, so Wordsworth felt, should be
ashamed to demand more obvious action. A narrative poet did well to
study spiritual victories.[2] The poetry in *The White Doe,* said Wordsworth, came as it should "from the soul of Man, communicating its
creative energies to the images of the external world." [3] Poetry should
come from the soul and should lead toward the illimitable. *The Excursion* had, he felt, "innumerable analogies and types of infinity"; the
images of sense in that poem held a relationship "to Immortality and
Infinity." [4] To Landor, who disliked books of religion, Wordsworth
wrote:

6. *The Prelude,* II, 317–22.
7. *Intimations* ode, ll. 149, 150.
8. *The Prelude,* VI, 604–8.
9. *The Prelude,* XI, 142–4.
1. Letter to Henry Reed, July 1, 1845, in *Wordsworth and Reed, the Poet's Correspondence with His American Editor: 1836–1850,* ed. Leslie Nathan Broughton (Ithaca,
Cornell University Press, 1933), p. 144.
2. *MY, 1,* 197–8.
3. *MY, 2,* 705.
4. *MY, 2,* 617–19.

I am afraid it is a bad sign in me, that I have little relish for any other
—even in poetry it is the imaginative only, viz., that which is conver-
sant [with], or turns upon infinity, that powerfully affects me,—
perhaps I ought to explain: I mean to say that, unless in those passages where things are lost in each other, and limits vanish, and as-
pirations are raised, I read with something too much like indifference
—but all great poets are in this view powerful Religionists.[5]

Central to both Wordsworth's interest in psychology and his interest
in religion is his awareness of the creative power of the mind. This imaginative, active power was what Wordsworth valued most. Imagination
is in truth

> but another name for absolute power
> And clearest insight, amplitude of mind,
> And Reason in her most exalted mood.[6]

Consequently he desired his own poems to be judged by "the powers
of mind they call forth, and the energies they presuppose and excite."
He valued his poems as "being *a new power* in the literary world." [7] He
delighted in the power which he was conscious of exerting; the poetry
should come not from the subject but from the mind. Ambitious that his
poems should transmit power, he addressed Coleridge:

> Forgive me if I say that I, who long
> Had harbour'd reverentially a thought
> That Poets, even as Prophets, each with each
> Connected in a mighty scheme of truth,
> Have each for his peculiar dower, a sense
> By which he is enabled to perceive
> Something unseen before; forgive me, Friend,
> If I, the meanest of this Band, had hope
> That unto me had also been vouchsafed
> An influx, that in some sort I possess'd
> A privilege, and that a work of mine,
> Proceeding from the depth of untaught things,
> Enduring and creative, might become
> A power like one of Nature's.[8]

5. *LY, I,* 134–5. This identification of the imaginative with the spiritual does much to
explain Wordsworth's disinterest in Jane Austen's novels. He found them an "admirable
copy of life" but not interesting because "the pervading light of imagination" was lacking. See letter of Sara Coleridge to Miss E. Trevenen, August, 1834, quoted in Batho,
The Later Wordsworth, p. 372.
6. *The Prelude,* XIV, 189–92.
7. *Diary, I,* 389, 482.
8. *The Prelude,* XII, A, 299–312.

Coleridge had previously, Wordsworth recalled, said of Wordsworth's lines written during his journey across the Plain of Sarum

> That also then I must have exercised
> Upon the vulgar forms of present things
> And actual world of our familiar days,
> A higher power.[9]

[Wordsworth's theory of poetry, then, develops the truth, passion, and power of poetry] His remarks about language lead even more directly into his theory of imagery.

The power of poetry came both from the mind of the poet and from the life inherent in language. Wordsworth thought of words not as lifeless things mechanically linked to objects or ideas but as living powers in their own right. He sent advice to the sister of William Hamilton, who had submitted her poems to his criticism, that she should improve "in the habit of looking at things through the steady light of words; and, to speak a little metaphysically, words are not a mere *vehicle,* but they are *powers* either to kill or to animate." [1] Language and the human mind act and react on each other; [2] the genius of the poet should shape for his own purposes "the endless fluctuations and arbitrary associations" of language. The creative energy of the mind could melt down and reshape words; [3] yet words remain a mystery to be respected.

The mystery of words was associated in Wordsworth's mind with the mystery of creative power. Speaking of his own response to "the great Nature that exists in works / Of mighty Poets," he commented:

> Visionary power
> Attends the motions of the viewless winds,
> Embodied in the mystery of words:
> There, darkness makes abode, and all the host
> Of shadowy things work endless changes,—there,
> As in a mansion like their proper home,
> Even forms and substances are circumfused
> By that transparent veil with light divine,
> And, through the turnings intricate of verse,
> Present themselves as objects recognized,
> In flashes, and with glory not their own.[4]

The poet breathes creative power into words, but words already possess a creative energy of their own. Words can kill or animate; they can illuminate or conceal. The "shadowy things" to which the poet must

9. *The Prelude,* xii, A, 360–3.
1. *LY, 1,* 437.
2. "Preface to the Lyrical Ballads," *PW, 2,* 385.
3. "Essay, Supplementary to the Preface (1815)," *PW, 2,* 428.
4. *The Prelude,* v, 595–605.

give life and form can come into being only through words; in and
through them "Even forms and substances" can be illuminated.[5] Wordsworth thought of writing as endowing "with a frame of outward life,"
as fixing "in a visible home" the phantoms that floated about homeless
and lifeless.[6] He was conscious that sometimes in his own writing when
he had seemed to himself to have created a sufficient memorial of his
experience he had in reality "scarcely . . . produced / A monument
and arbitrary sign." Adequately to convey his meaning required

> That patience which, admitting no neglect
> By slow creation, doth impart(s) to speach
> Outline and substance even, till it has given
> A function kindred to organic power,
> The vital spirit of a perfect form.[7]

Words were mysterious instruments capable of taking on outline and
substance, coming by slow creation to possess "The vital spirit of a
perfect form."

Because of his concern for what is at once real and ideal, for truth
rooted in fact and suggesting the spiritual, Wordsworth was, however, highly critical of language that in any way attracted attention to
itself at the expense of the truth of thought and feeling. Minute criticism, he knew, was irksome, "Yet every mind must occasionally be ex-
ercised in this discipline, else it cannot learn the art of bringing words
rigorously to the test of thoughts; and these again to a comparison with
things, their archetypes, contemplated first in themselves, and secondly
in relation to each other." [8] Wordsworth's three essays on epitaphs alike
elaborate his conviction that thought should not be regarded as independent of the form in which it is expressed, a conviction which antici-
pates the contemporary doctrine of the identity of form and content.
Protesting against false and artificial expressions in epitaphs, Wordsworth laments the absence of "those thoughts which have the infinitude
of truth, and those expressions which are not what the garb is to the
body but what the body is to the soul, themselves a constituent part and
power or function in the thought." Wordsworth himself thought that
in an epitaph "the affections, the memory, and the imagination would

5. It is interesting to read this passage in connection with the passages in the first book
of *The Prelude*, ll. 380–400, in which Wordsworth recounts how when he had stolen a
boat the very mountains seemed to pursue him. Afterward, he says, "my brain /
Worked with a dim and undetermined sense / Of unknown modes of being." A darkness
fell on his thoughts, and "huge and mighty forms" troubled his dreams. It is significant,
I think, that in the next lines, 401–4, Wordsworth apostrophizes the "Wisdom and
Spirit of the universe . . . That gives to forms and images a breath / And everlasting
motion." In both passages the creative genius calls from darkness "shadowy things"; in
both passages creative energy makes "forms and substances" take on life.

6. *The Prelude*, I, A, 123–33.

7. *The Prelude*, p. xliii, from an autograph MS of 1798–1800.

8. "Upon Epitaphs," *Prose Works, 2,* 57.

be *constrained* to speak their genuine language," but actual specimens of epitaphs showed, he found, that from the great desire of the author to do justice to the occasion the faults of expression of the literature of any age were more evident in epitaphs than in other kinds of verse.[9] Some instances show true feeling lost under false illustrative imagery; others show a want even of true feeling, with thoughts and feelings in "no vital union, but . . . artificially connected, or formally accumulated." [1] His point is clearly that there should be no such separation of thought and expression. Bad taste alone accounts for such disparity.

> Words are too awful an instrument for good and evil, to be trifled with; they hold above all other external powers a dominion over thoughts. If words be not (recurring to a metaphor before used) an incarnation of the thought, but only a clothing for it, then surely will they prove an ill gift; such a one as those possessed vestments, read of in the stories of superstitious times, which had power to consume and to alienate from his right mind the victim who put them on. Language, if it do not uphold, and feed, and leave in quiet, like the power of gravitation or the air we breathe, is a counter-spirit, unremittingly and noiselessly at work, to subvert, to lay waste, to vitiate, and to dissolve.[2]

Wordsworth's much disputed remarks about the language of poetry should, it seems to me, be related to this discussion of the language of epitaphs. The words should be "an incarnation of the thought"; otherwise they were powers for evil. Consequently he felt that the language of poetry should be the real language of men; it should not be conventional, artificial language tricked out to please without relation to the thought. His insistence that there was no *essential* difference between the language of prose and the language of poetry likewise springs from his dislike of artificial, conventional expressions: the author of the epitaph in which genuine feeling underlies fantastic images must have been misled by a belief that "what was natural in prose would be out of place in verse" and that it was "the garb which makes the Muse." Therefore the misguided writer considered that the more unnatural his language, the more he honored the dead.[3] Artificial distinctions of style can only falsify and render ridiculous; the wise poet will select from real language and by selection achieve a sufficient dignity of language. "He will feel that there is no necessity to trick out or to elevate nature: and, the more industriously he applies this principle, the deeper will be his faith that no words which *his* fancy or imagination can suggest, will be to be

9. P. 64.
1. P. 62.
2. P. 65.
3. P. 52.

compared with those which are the emanations of reality and truth." [4]

The prolonged controversy that has sprung from Wordsworth's statement that "there neither is, nor can be, any *essential* difference between the language of prose and metrical composition" [5] has its origin, in my opinion, in the fact that Wordsworth made no clear distinction between words and the use of words and by "language" meant almost invariably not only words but the figures that words convey. In the "Advertisement" of 1798 announcing that the majority of the poems were written "chiefly with a view to ascertain how far the language of conversation in the middle and lower classes of society is adapted to the purposes of poetic pleasure," Wordsworth contrasts this language with "the gaudiness and inane phraseology of many modern writers." [6] In the "Preface to the Lyrical Ballads" of 1800, in a discussion of the style of his poems he rejects personifications of abstract ideas "as an ordinary device to elevate the style," since such personifications are no part of the real language of men. [7] For the same reason he has avoided traditional poetic diction. His endeavor to look steadily at the subject and avoid falsehood in description has cut him off "from a large portion of phrases and figures of speech which from father to son have long been regarded as the common inheritance of Poets." [8]

It is not surprising that Wordsworth's use of the term "language" is ambiguous. Wordsworth had learned from Hartley that all language is vitally metaphorical. Hartley's theory that all intellectual ideas arise from images of sense, simple ideas leading into complex ones by means of association, helps, I think, to explain the overtones that "language" had for Wordsworth. According to Hartley, figurative words and phrases rise by association; and by use, common figures fade out into literal words. [9] Only in the light of Hartley's doctrine can one understand Wordsworth's statement that in low and rustic life "the passions

4. "Preface to the Lyrical Ballads," *PW, 2,* 394. Passage added in 1802.

5. "Preface to the Lyrical Ballads," p. 392. Passage added in 1802. Wordsworth's defenders have tended to maintain that he meant only that there is no essential difference in the vocabularies of prose and poetry: see H. W. Garrod, *Wordsworth: Lectures and Essays* (Oxford, Clarendon Press, 1923), p. 163; Legouis, *The Early Life of William Wordsworth,* p. 445; and the comments of Coleridge's editors in Samuel Taylor Coleridge, *Biographia Literaria,* ed. J. Shawcross (Oxford, Clarendon Press, 1907), *2,* 276, and in Coleridge, *Biographia Literaria,* and Wordsworth, *Prefaces and Essays of Poetry, 1800–1815,* ed. George Sampson (Cambridge, The University Press, 1920), p. 304. Coleridge believed Wordsworth to be denying that there is any essential difference in the construction and order of the sentences and in the use and selection of figures of speech: *Biographia Literaria,* 2, 46–9, 69, 77. Marjorie Latta Barstow [Greenbie] in her study *Wordsworth's Theory of Poetic Diction* (New Haven, Yale University Press, 1917), pp. 134–5, dismissed both vocabulary and syntax as elements in Wordsworth's meaning and believed, as I do, that he was primarily interested in poetic imagery.

6. *PW, 2,* 383.

7. *PW, 2,* 390. Wording of 1802.

8. "Preface to the Lyrical Ballads," *PW, 2,* 390.

9. Hartley, *Observations on Man, 1,* 56, 73, 291–2.

of men are incorporated with the beautiful and permanent forms of nature." Wordsworth adopted the language of these men "because such men hourly communicate with the best objects from which the best part of language is originally derived." Such a language,

> arising out of repeated experience and regular feelings, is a more permanent, and a far more philosophical language, than that which is frequently substituted for it by Poets, who think that they are conferring honour upon themselves and their art, in proportion as they separate themselves from the sympathies of men, and indulge in arbitrary and capricious habits of expression, in order to furnish food for fickle tastes, and fickle appetites, of their own creation.[1]

Wordsworth, then, was trying to return poetic imagery to a basis in common and permanent experience. The poet who used secondhand conventions inevitably falsified what he wrote of; the simple peasant who lived among mountains and sheep associated a clear image with such ideas. Metaphors based on firsthand experience would be clear and real. "I do not know how to give my Reader a more exact notion of the style in which it was my wish and intention to write," said Wordsworth, "than by informing him that I have at all times endeavoured to look steadily at my subject." [2] Imagery like poetry itself should be *true*.

It becomes clear too why Wordsworth felt that there should be no essential difference between the language of prose and of poetry. The poet needs less stimulus than other men to think and to feel and has greater power of expression. But his passions and thoughts and feelings are "the general passions and thoughts and feelings of men." They are connected like those of other men with the seasons and the weather, with affections and experiences. "The Poet thinks and feels in the spirit of human passions. How, then, can his language differ in any material degree from that of all other men who feel vividly and see clearly?" Poetry to Wordsworth was truth "carried alive into the heart by passion." Its language should be based on real experience and knowledge, not on arbitrary and capricious habits of expression. Fundamentally Wordsworth was attacking the concept of imagery as ornament: "it is not . . . to be supposed that any one, who holds that sublime notion of Poetry which I have attempted to convey, will break in upon the sanctity and truth of his pictures by transitory and accidental ornaments, and endeavour to excite admiration of himself by arts, the necessity of which must manifestly depend upon the assumed meanness of his subject." [3]

Since poetry originated in feeling and feeling made the truth of poetry

1. "Preface to the Lyrical Ballads," *PW, 2,* 387.
2. "Preface to the Lyrical Ballads," p. 390.
3. "Preface to the Lyrical Ballads," pp. 397–8. Addition of 1802.

alive and operative, feeling was always the test of figurative imagery. The earliest poets used figurative language because they wrote from genuine passion. Any poet who chose his subject judiciously would find that it would naturally lead him to figurative imagery. Such passages "which with propriety abound with metaphors and figures" will prove more effective "if, upon other occasions where the passions are of a milder character, the style also be subdued and temperate." [4]

[Figurative imagery which did not rise from genuine feeling was in Wordsworth's opinion vicious.] Poetic diction, by which Wordsworth meant the "mechanical adoption" of figures of speech, was "arbitrary and subject to infinite caprices"; the only thing it had in common with the genuine language of poetry was "that it was not heard in ordinary conversation." It had arisen, Wordsworth thought, when poets wished to make an effect without themselves being moved by real feeling. Unfortunately readers had come to identify this unnatural language with poetry and to expect it; [5] were they more familiar with the older English poets, however, they would complain less of simple language. [6]

Rightly, all images should originate "in that sane state of feeling which arises out of thought" and they should "excite thought or feeling in the Reader." The great trouble with Johnson's parody of the *Babes in the Wood* was its want of sense: its images neither came from feeling nor led to any thought or feeling. [7] Poetic imagery ought always to "elevate, deepen, or refine the human passion" or it should not act at all. [8] Feeling and imagery should be consonant: Wordsworth's whole discussion of the artificial style common to epitaphs of the preceding century emphasizes repeatedly the necessity for a harmony of thought and feeling and expression. Pope's epitaphs Wordsworth condemned not only for lacking necessary common feeling but for being contrived and false. Wordsworth wished to help the reader separate "truth and sincerity from falsehood and affectation. [9] Ideally "images and sentiments" should be "wedded" in the mind; images should not be artificial, the result of a strained effort to impress; they should come unsought for, rising up in the mind like "exhalations." [1] Especially "in lyric poetry the subject and simile should be as much as possible lost in each other." [2]

While images should come unsought for, inspired by feeling, they nevertheless are the work of the imagination. Figurative imagery differs from literal imagery in involving this activity of the mind: direct

4. "Preface to the Lyrical Ballads," pp. 392–3. Addition of 1802.
5. Appendix of 1802, *PW, 2,* 405–6.
6. "Advertisement" of 1798, *PW, 2,* 383–4.
7. "Preface to the Lyrical Ballads," *PW, 2,* 402–3.
8. "Upon Epitaphs," *Prose Works, 2,* 56.
9. "Upon Epitaphs," pp. 60, 62.
1. "Letter to Mathetes," *Prose Works, 1,* 318. Cf. *The Prelude,* IV, 113–14.
2. *LY, 1,* 158–9.

imagery (what I term literal imagery) appears "under the shape of description or incident"; metaphor is "collateral . . . colouring the style"; simile is "illustrative." [3] Wordsworth's describing the simile as "illustrative" perhaps reflects the influence of eighteenth-century thinking, but he understood, as the eighteenth century did not, that imagery determines meaning. A poet's expressions, as we have seen, should be "a constituent part and power or function in the thought." [4]

The imagination, as Wordsworth defines the word, becomes the name for the mental power that transforms the literal to the figurative. It "has no reference to images that are merely a faithful copy, existing in the mind, of absent external objects; but is a word of higher import, denoting operations of the mind upon those objects, and processes of creation or of composition, governed by certain fixed laws." [5] Clarence Thorpe holds that when Wordsworth comes to explain these laws he falls back on principles of association.[6] This, it seems to me, is exactly what Wordsworth does not do: his whole point is the process of creation—the power of the mind to do more than associate mechanically. The mind can confer on objects properties not inherent in them, it can abstract from them some of the properties that they actually possess, and it can modify one image by another.[7] In every case the mind alters the object creatively.

Wordsworth shows by examples the way in which the imagination may be exerted upon images independent of one another. Quoting Milton's lines

> As when far off at sea a fleet described
> *Hangs* in the clouds, by equinoctial winds
> Close sailing from Bengala, or the isles
> Of Ternate or Tidore, whence merchants bring
> Their spicy drugs; they on the trading flood
> Through the wide Ethiopian to the Cape
> Ply, stemming nightly toward the Pole: so seemed
> Far off the flying Fiend.[8]

Wordsworth comments:

> Here is the full strength of the imagination involved in the word *hangs,* and exerted upon the whole image: First, the fleet, an aggregate of many ships, is represented as one mighty person, whose track, we know and feel, is upon the waters; but, taking advantage of its ap-

---

3. *MY, 2,* 617. See also "Conversations and Reminiscences as Recorded by the (Now) Bishop of Lincoln," *Prose Works, 3,* 464.
4. See above, p. 130; n. 9, p. 131.
5. "Preface to the Edition of 1815," *PW, 2,* 436.
6. "The Imagination: Coleridge *versus* Wordsworth," *PQ, 18* (January, 1939), 1–18.
7. "Preface to the Edition of 1815," p. 436.
8. *Paradise Lost,* ii, 636–43.

pearance to the senses, the Poet dares to represent it as *hanging in the clouds,* both for the gratification of the mind in contemplating the image itself, and in reference to the motion and appearance of the sublime objects to which it is compared.[9]

Here the fleet in being made to hang not only is endowed with a quality that it does not literally have but is creatively unified into one body. The imagination can call in the affections to assist in conveying a particular quality or can express a complex idea by means of metaphor. In discussing the action of the imagination "employed upon images in a conjunction by which they modify each other" Wordsworth quotes from his own *Resolution and Independence* the passage which compares the man to a stone and the stone to a sea beast, and comments on the interaction of the images.[1]

Wordsworth, it is clear, regarded such images not as being mechanical juxtapositions but as involving creative interaction. The stone, the sea beast, and the old man act and react upon one another to convey the sense of the old man's kinship with primordial nature. The interaction, it should be noticed, in no way falsifies either the stone, the sea beast, or the man but rather expresses the poet's vision of the man.

Essentially, the endowing, abstracting, and modifying powers are creative. Wordsworth is somewhat confusing as he proceeds: "Thus far of an endowing or modifying power: but the Imagination also shapes and *creates;* and how? By innumerable processes; and in none does it more delight than in that of consolidating numbers into unity, and dissolving and separating unity into number,—alternations proceeding from, and governed by, a sublime consciousness of the soul in her own mighty and almost divine powers." [2] This statement sounds, as Havens observes,[3] as if the "endowing or modifying power" was not creative. The truth seems to be that Wordsworth is simply giving additional emphasis to the power of the imagination to produce a new vision. He recurs at once to the image of Milton's previously cited as an instance of the endowing or modifying power, and as a second instance of the creative power he refers again to Milton: "Hear again this mighty Poet, —speaking of the Messiah going forth to expel from heaven the rebellious angels,

> "Attended by ten thousand thousand Saints
> He onward came: far off his coming shone,"—

9. "Preface to the Edition of 1815," p. 437. John L. Lowes, "Wordsworth and Goldsmith," *The Nation, 92* (March, 1911), 289–90, has pointed out the parallel between this passage of Wordsworth's and Goldsmith's discussion of *pendere* in his essay "Poetry Distinguished from Other Writing" (No. 15).
1. "Preface to the Edition of 1815," *PW, 2,* 438.
2. "Preface to the Edition of 1815," pp. 438–9.
3. Havens, *The Mind of a Poet,* p. 210.

the retinue of Saints, and the Person of the Messiah himself, lost almost and merged in the splendour of that indefinite abstraction 'His coming!' " [4] Since the first of Milton's images at once endows and creates and the second both abstracts and creates, Wordsworth seems to mean that the imagination unifies and creates in connection with its powers of conferring, abstracting, and modifying.

In Wordsworth's opinion both the imagination and the fancy aggregate and associate, evoke and combine; the difference is that the fancy makes no pretense to truth in its combinations and that nothing happens to things combined by the fancy. The resemblances framed by the imagination depend "less upon outline of form and feature, than upon expression and effect; less upon casual and outstanding, than upon inherent and internal, properties: moreover, the images invariably modify each other." [5] Such comparisons, based on profound resemblances, are the product of the mind in its activity. Wordsworth seems here to have anticipated present-day psychiatry in the knowledge that some things have a natural symbolic function. The universal language that enables a physician to understand the core of the patient's problem long before the patient himself has consciously grasped it is also the language of the profoundest and truest poetry. Imaginative images are those in which the nature of things sustains the combination. Images produced by the fancy are not supported by this universal language and are consequently superficial.

The significance of Wordsworth's insistence on the truth, passion, and power of both poetry and imagery seems very great indeed. His statement that "a practical faith in the opinions which I am wishing to establish is almost unknown" [6] was not the exaggeration that it may seem. The simple statement that the materials of poetry "are to be found in every subject which can interest the human mind" understood in its full ramifications attacks not only the concept of poetry long current but the whole philosophic-scientific understanding of the nature of the universe and of the human mind. The Hobbes-Locke-Hume tradition had firmly established a concept of the universe as a great mechanism operating according to fixed and ascertainable laws, and of the mind as a comparable mechanism passively accepting what was given to it through the senses and forming ideas by association. Language consisted of an arbitrary system of signs each of which had its proper meaning. Poetry was decorative and ornamental, and figurative language was a way of dressing up objects not intrinsically pleasing enough to be poetic otherwise. Wordsworth left none of this untouched. Strongly imbued with a sense of a living, active universe, familiar by experience

---

4. *Paradise Lost*, vi, 767–8. "Preface to the Edition of 1815," p. 439.
5. "Preface to the Edition of 1815," p. 441.
6. "Preface to the Lyrical Ballads," *PW*, *2*, 393.

with the power of the mind to act upon reality, Wordsworth tended to think of consciousness as being born of the marriage of the mind with the universe.[7] The process is reciprocal: eye and ear half create and half perceive. The same spirit that is interfused in "the living air / And the blue sky" dwells also "in the mind of man." [8] Language like the mind has a life of its own: the two act and react on each other. The creative life in language and the creative power in the mind alike find their completest expression in poetry. Far from being mere tacked-on ornament, figurative imagery is the consequence of the creative power of the mind acting upon objects. Poetry is creative; the life of the universe stimulates the life of the mind; poetry comes not from any object or subject as such but from the meeting of object and mind in language.

Wordsworth in regarding figurative imagery as the consequence of the operation of mind upon objects seems to be on firmer ground than are the critics who now dispute the relative importance of thought and feeling as associative links in imagery. Never does Wordsworth concern himself with the question of whether imaginative links express primarily the emotions or the intellect: he has too sound an understanding of the connection between thought and feeling. What to the critic may seem thoughts *and* feelings in the mind of the poet is one matrix: Wordsworth tends to speak always of "thought and feeling and imagery" as one individual whole.[9] In "Over his own sweet voice the stock-dove *broods*" the metaphor "broods" calls in the affections by the imagination to help mark "the manner in which the bird reiterates and prolongs her soft note." [1] In most of the images he discusses, Wordsworth emphasizes primarily the idea being expressed. It is curious in the light of Wordsworth's analysis of the way the mind functions in images to recall that he is supposed by recent critics to be hostile to the play of mind in imagery. It is likewise curious in the light of his insistence on the activity of the mind to find him placed among those who believed poetry to reside in specific poetic objects.

The very fact that Wordsworth's remarks about imagery are so inextricably connected with his remarks about the imagination and about language reveals the profundity of his insight. Early in his life aesthetics and poetics were sometimes lost sight of in psychology; late in his life aesthetics and poetics were subordinate to religion; yet in all periods Wordsworth looked for creative power in poetry. Recognizing the limitations of the abstracting intellect, he looked in poetry for the wisdom of the heart and the grandeur of the imagination. The poet is the man "who rejoices more than other men in the spirit of life that is in him"; [2]

---

7. Prospectus to *The Excursion*, ll. 52–71.
8. *Tintern Abbey*, ll. 95–107.
9. *MY*, *1*, 78; see also p. 125.
1. "Preface to the Edition of 1815," *PW*, *2*, 437.
2. "Preface to the Lyrical Ballads," p. 393.

he is the man in whom the creative spirit has not died under the burden of abstract thought; he is able to see life whole.

Wordsworth's best poetry clearly has the wholeness of vision—the imaginative truth, passion, and power that Wordsworth's theory demands. At its best the Wordsworthian landscape holds in one vision the dark sense of the burden of the mystery and the bright sense of redeeming love; Wordsworth's people at their best are either solitary sufferers who in their anguish embody the human predicament and the human achievement or solitary wanderers who in their uncanny quiet suggest another world. Sounds suggest the invisible; waters image the currents of emotion, thought, and life itself; man-made structures image both the perishability of the temporal and the imperishability of the city of the soul. The vision is at once tragic and religious; pain and anguish are not denied and yet reality is divine. Wordsworth's unique position in English poetry results from his seeking in theory and achieving in practice the transfiguration of the commonplace by the divine.

But while Wordsworth's poetry fulfills his theory, it is less certain that the theory altogether accounts for the poetry. Wordsworth's best images are symbols, but he advances no explicit theory of symbolism. His discussion of the relation of fact to poetic truth, of the common transmuted, of the individual form which is both real and true [3] does, however, point directly to the symbol. Crabb Robinson, who could not comprehend Wordsworth's ideas concerning the poetic imagination, understood that "imagination is the faculty by which the poet conceives and produces—that is, images—individual forms, in which are embodied universal ideas or abstractions." [4] Robinson, of course, has here defined the poetic symbol, the individual form, the yellow primrose that is a primrose and something more. Certainly throughout Wordsworth's remarks on poetic theory there is constant stress on the power of the imagination to transform the familiar.

More serious is the fact that Wordsworth's theory was, as everyone has observed, capable of damaging his poetry. Theory seems to have been responsible for the original and much ridiculed verses in *The Thorn:*

> I've measured it from side to side;
> 'Tis three feet long, and two feet wide.[5]

Theory seems to have been responsible for Simon Lee's swollen ankles and for the emphasis in *The Idiot Boy* on the maternal passion. Theory seems to have been responsible for the changes in the original form of *The Ruined Cottage.* At times one can only conclude that Wordsworth

3. See above, p. 118.
4. *Diary,* 2, 25.
5. *PW, 2, apparatus criticus,* 241.

did not know his own strength and confused his theories with his poetic powers.

Such reservations, however, cannot diminish Wordsworth's very real contributions to poetic theory. [In his insistence on the imagination as a creative power born of strong feeling and deep thought, in his insistence on the functional nature of imagery, in his insistence on the union of thought and feeling and imagery in creative activity, Wordsworth was restoring poetry to its birthright. On these points his theory seems valid not only for his own poetry but for all poetry.]

Index